Mastering
Industrial-Organizational Psychology

THE SIOP PROFESSIONAL PRACTICE SERIES

Series Editor
Nancy T. Tippins

Mastering
Industrial-Organizational Psychology

*Training Issues for Master's Level
I-O Psychologists*

Edited by

ELIZABETH L. SHOENFELT

Published in partnership with

OXFORD
UNIVERSITY PRESS

Oxford University Press is a department of the University of Oxford. It furthers the University's objective of excellence in research, scholarship, and education by publishing worldwide. Oxford is a registered trade mark of Oxford University Press in the UK and certain other countries.

Published in the United States of America by Oxford University Press
198 Madison Avenue, New York, NY 10016, United States of America.

Library of Congress Cataloging-in-Publication Data
Names: Shoenfelt, Elizabeth L., editor.
Title: Mastering industrial-organizational psychology : training issues for
master's level I-O psychologists / edited by Elizabeth L. Shoenfelt.
Description: New York, NY : Oxford University Press, [2020] |
Series: The SIOP professional practice |
Includes bibliographical references and index.
Identifiers: LCCN 2020004538 (print) | LCCN 2020004539 (ebook) |
ISBN 9780190071141 (hardback) | ISBN 9780190071165 (epub) |
ISBN 9780197529218
Subjects: LCSH: Psychology, Industrial—Study and teaching (Higher) |
Psychology, Industrial—Vocational guidance. |
Industrial psychologists—Training of.
Classification: LCC HF5548.8 .M376 2020 (print) | LCC HF5548.8 (ebook) |
DDC 158.7—dc23
LC record available at https://lccn.loc.gov/2020004538
LC ebook record available at https://lccn.loc.gov/2020004539

1 3 5 7 9 8 6 4 2

Printed by Integrated Books International, United States of America

Contents

Preface

I was honored when the Professional Practice Series Committee of the Society for Industrial and Organizational Psychology (SIOP) invited me to propose and then edit this book, *Mastering Industrial-Organizational Psychology: Training Issues for Master's Level I-O Psychologists*, and its sister volume, *Mastering the Job Market: Career Issues for Master's Level Industrial-Organizational Psychologists*, both focusing on master's-level industrial-organizational (I-O) issues. The field of I-O psychology has been spotlighted recently by the U.S. Bureau of Labor statistics as one of the fastest-growing occupations in the nation (ABC News, 2014) and continues to be recognized as a top job (U.S. Bureau of Labor Statistics, 2019). Master's-level graduate training programs in I-O psychology have exponentially increased in number over the past several decades, with fewer than 20 in the early 1980s to more than 170 currently listed on the SIOP website (SIOP, 2019). I-O master's programs now outnumber doctoral programs and produce a larger number of graduates. Concomitantly with the growth in master's programs, SIOP has devoted more resources and attention to master's issues, as evidenced by these two books in the SIOP Professional Practice Series. When I contacted I-O master's program directors and faculty to serve as authors of the books, they shared my excitement and enthusiasm for the books focused on I-O master's training and careers. This, the first book, provides best practices for I-O master's training and education from faculty in some of the top I-O master's programs in the nation.

Purpose and Audience

Mastering Industrial-Organizational Psychology: Training Issues for Master's Level I-O Psychologists targets three audiences. First, the book will provide valuable guidance to faculty in I-O master's programs. With the growth of master's programs, faculty are eager to learn the ropes of running a master's program. The sessions on master's issues at the SIOP annual conference are well attended, frequently with standing room only. This volume consolidates best practices from authors with decades of experience and an abundance of tacit knowledge regarding the components of successful I-O master's programs. The insights provided should prove invaluable to newer faculty in I-O master's programs as well as for more senior faculty in their efforts to make their program one of the best.

Second, SIOP members lament that I-O psychology is not well known to those outside the discipline (e.g., Ryan, 2003), even by other psychologists (Gasser, Whitsett, Mosley, Sullivan, Rogers, & Tan, 1998). Accordingly, many psychology faculty in departments without an I-O psychologist are unaware of careers in I-O psychology as they advise promising undergraduates about graduate school and careers. It is not unusual for graduate students in my I-O master's program to speak of the serendipitous manner in which they learned of I-O psychology. This volume will assist with advising undergraduates and will inform advisors about graduate training in I-O psychology, hopefully bringing interested students into the field of I-O psychology.

Our third audience comprises those students who are interested in earning a graduate degree and then in a career in I-O psychology. Our book will provide these prospective students with information on applying to graduate school and what they should look for in an I-O graduate program to ensure a successful graduate school experience.

Overview of the Volume

Mastering Industrial-Organizational Psychology: Training Issues for Master's Level I-O Psychologists begins with an introduction to the field of I-O psychology and a discussion of issues related to I-O master's training by Shoenfelt, Hays-Thomas, and Koppes Bryan. Stone and Sanders then provide direction for applying to graduate programs, selecting a program that is the right fit for the applicant, and undergraduate experiences needed to prepare for graduate school. In Chapter 3, Huelsman and Shanock discuss the competencies identified in the SIOP (2016) *Guidelines for Education and Training in Industrial-Organizational Psychology*, a variety of methods for teaching these competencies, and opportunities and challenges for I-O master's programs with different characteristics. Next, Kottke, Shultz, and Aamodt discuss the importance of applied experiences in training I-O master's students, most of whom become applied I-O practitioners, and provide examples of applied experiences such as internships, practica, and applied course projects.

In Chapter 5, Schneider and Mullins discuss the pros, cons, and feasibility of thesis projects and provide guidance on traversing Institutional Review Board requirements and on-time thesis completion. Sachau and Fritzsche then provide insight on issues faced by faculty in I-O master's programs with helpful advice for balancing the demands of teaching, research, and service. Finally, in Chapter 7, Hein, Moffett, and Nakai provide insight and advice about on-campus consulting centers affiliated with an I-O master's program that inform whether to develop such a center and how to maintain it. It is my hope that you find this book interesting, informative, and useful.

Elizabeth L. Shoenfelt

References

ABC News. (2014). https://abcnews.go.com/Business/americas-20-fastest-growing-jobs-surprise/story?id=22364716

Gasser, M., Whitsett, D., Mosley, N., Sullivan, K., Rogers, T., & Tan, R. (1998). I-O Psychology: What's your line? *The Industrial-Organizational Psychologist, 35*(4), 120–126. https://doi.org/10.1037/e577062011-013

Ryan, A. M. (2003). Defining ourselves: I-O psychology's identity quest. *The Industrial-Organizational Psychologist, 41*(1), 21–33. https://doi.org/10.1037/e578792011-002

Society for Industrial and Organizational Psychology, Inc. (2016). *Guidelines for education and training in industrial-organizational psychology*. Bowling Green, OH: Author. https://www.siop.org/Events-Education/Graduate-Training-Program/Guidelines-for-Education-and-Training

Society for Industrial and Organizational Psychology, Inc. (2019). http://siop.org/GTP/

U.S. Bureau of Labor Statistics (2019). Occupational employment statistics. https://www.bls.gov/oes/current/oes193032.htm

Contributors

Michael G. Aamodt, PhD
Principal Consultant
DCI Consulting Group, Inc.
Pulaski, VA

Laura Koppes Bryan, PhD
T. G. Lewis Faculty Scholar in
Organizational Behavior
Lewis Honors College
University of Kentucky
Lexington, KY

Barbara A. Fritzsche, PhD
Associate Dean
College of Graduate Studies
University of Central Florida
Orlando, FL

Rosemary Hays-Thomas, PhD
Professor, Emerita
Department of Psychology
University of West Florida
New Orleans, LA

Michael Hein, PhD
Professor & Director
Department of Psychology
Middle Tennessee State University
Murfreesboro, TN

Timothy J. Huelsman, PhD
Professors and Program Director
Department of Psychology
Appalachian State University
Boone, NC

Janet L. Kottke, PhD
Professor
Department of Psychology
California State University,
San Bernardino
San Bernardino, CA

Richard G. Moffett III, PhD
Professor
Department of Psychology
Middle Tennessee State University
Murfreesboro, TN

Morrie Mullins, PhD
Professor, Industrial-Organizational
Psychology
Department of Psychology
Xavier University
Loveland, OH

Yoshie Nakai, PhD
Associate Professor
Department of Psychology
Eastern Kentucky University
Lexington, KY

Daniel A. Sachau, PhD
Professor
Department of Psychology
Minnesota State University
Madison Lake, MN

Adriane M. F. Sanders, PhD
Director, MSIO Psychology Program &
Associate Professor
Department of Psychological Science
and Counseling
Austin Peay State University
Clarksville, TN

Kimberly T. Schneider, PhD
Associate Professor
Department of Psychology
Illinois State University
Bloomington, IL

Linda Rhoades Shanock, PhD
Professor
Department of Psychological Science
University of North Carolina Charlotte
Hendersonville, NC

Elizabeth L. Shoenfelt, PhD
University Distinguished Professor
Department of Psychological Sciences
Western Kentucky University
Bowling Green, KY

Kenneth S. Shultz, PhD
Professor
Department of Psychology
California State University,
San Bernardino
Claremont, CA

Nancy J. Stone, PhD
Professor
Department of Psychological Science
Missouri University of Science and
Technology
Rolla, MO

Author Biographies

Michael G. Aamodt is a Principal Consultant for DCI Consulting Group, Inc. He spends most of his days conducting salary equity analyses, computing adverse impact statistics, and helping develop employee selection systems for federal contractors and other organizations. Prior to working for DCI, Mike spent 26 years as a professor of Industrial/Organizational Psychology at Radford University. He received his BA in psychology from Pepperdine University in Malibu, California, and both his MA and PhD from the University of Arkansas. Mike has published several books in the human resources area, published over 60 research articles and book chapters, and presented over 150 papers at professional conferences. He was the 1991 winner of the Radford University Excellence in Teaching Award.

Laura Koppes Bryan, T. G. Lewis Faculty Scholar in Organizational Behavior of the Lewis Honors College, University of Kentucky, earned her PhD in I-O Psychology from The Ohio State University. She is a U.S. Fulbright Scholar and Fellow of the American Psychological Association, Association for Psychological Science, and Society for Industrial-Organizational Psychology. Previously, she was the Vice President for Academic Affairs/Dean of the University for Transylvania University, a nationally ranked private liberal arts institution. She secured funding for faculty and student success including grants from the Andrew W. Mellon Foundation, National Science Foundation, Alfred P. Sloan Foundation, State University System of Florida, Jesse Ball duPont Fund, and Bingham Trust. She authored *Shaping Work-Life Culture in Higher Education: A Guide for Academic Leaders* and coauthored *EEO Law and Personnel Practices*. She edited the scholarly text *Historical Perspectives in Industrial-Organizational Psychology* and co-edited *Using I-O Psychology for the Greater Good: Helping Those Who Help Others*.

Barbara A. Fritzsche received her PhD from the University of South Florida and is currently Associate Dean of Graduate Studies at the University of Central Florida (UCF). She has 16 years of administrative experience at UCF including Associate Chair of the Department of Psychology, I-O MS

Program Director, and I-O PhD Program Director. Her research interests include the aging workforce and workplace wellness programs. She has won several teaching awards including the College of Sciences Excellence in Graduate Teaching Award. She serves on the editorial board for the *Journal of Organizational Behavior* and has published over 40 papers in outlets such as *Journal of Vocational Behavior; Work, Aging, and Retirement; Journal of Management; Human Resource Management; Journal of World Business*; and *Journal of Occupational and Organizational Psychology*.

Rosemary Hays-Thomas, SPHR, earned her master's and doctorate in Social Psychology at the University of Illinois Urbana-Champaign. After teaching and conducting program evaluation research, she completed postdoctoral work in I-O Psychology at LSU, then joined the faculty of the University of West Florida, where she coordinated the I-O Master's track and was Department Chair. She was an active member of SIOP and the Southeastern Psychological Association, in which she held elected offices and served as Administrative Officer. She is a member of APA, APS, and SHRM, and a Fellow of APA Divisions 2, 9, and 35. While at UWF, she was Board Member and Chair of the Council of Applied Master's Programs in Psychology (CAMPP) and represented graduate department chairs at APA's Board of Educational Affairs. She has published and presented on master's issues and is the author of a recent text on the psychology of managing workforce diversity.

Michael Hein is the Director of the Center for Organizational and Human Resource Effectiveness (COHRE) and a Professor of Psychology at Middle Tennessee State University (MTSU). He received his PhD in Industrial-Organizational (I-O) Psychology from Georgia Institute of Technology in 1990. He has over 30 years of experience consulting with clients in a variety of industries on projects regarding job analysis, employee surveys, training, onboarding, leadership development, and organizational performance measurement. His research interests include leadership, best use of training-practice time, the determinants of skilled task performance, and the development of expertise. Dr. Hein has taught in several areas of I-O psychology, research design, and statistics such as job performance and appraisal, training, research methodology, and factor analysis. He was awarded the MTSU 2016 Career Achievement Award. He is a member of the Society for Industrial and Organizational Psychology and the American Psychological Society.

Timothy J. Huelsman is a Professor of Psychology at Appalachian State University where he has directed the Industrial-Organizational Psychology and Human Resource Management master's program since 2003. He has taught graduate and undergraduate courses in organizational psychology, program evaluation, research methods, statistics, and personality. His research and consulting interests include organizational culture and climate, strategic planning, personality and mood, and organizational assessment. Tim is a past Chairperson of the North Carolina I-O Psychologists and, as a member of the Society for Industrial and Organizational Psychology, he co-authored the current *Guidelines for Education and Training in Industrial-Organizational Psychology* and participated in the creation of the annual Master's Student Consortium. Tim was presented with the University of North Carolina Board of Governors Award for Excellence in Teaching in 2014 and was inducted into Appalachian State University's Academy of Outstanding Graduate Mentors in 2013.

Janet L. Kottke is a Professor of Psychology at California State University, San Bernardino (CSUSB). She earned her MS and PhD in Industrial and Organizational (I-O) Psychology from Iowa State University. Jan founded the I-O master's program at CSUSB, has served as its Director, externship coordinator, student group advisor, and outcome assessment director. She has published frequently in *Teaching of Psychology* and has presented numerous papers at national conferences on pedagogical issues, especially at the master's level. She won the 2008–2009 Outstanding Professor Award at CSUSB, which recognizes excellence in teaching, research, and service. In 2019, she was elected a Fellow of the Society for the Teaching of Psychology, Division 2 of the American Psychological Association, and was the recipient of the 2020 Distinguished Teaching Contributions Award, given by the Society for Industrial and Organizational Psychology.

Richard G. Moffett III is the current Associate Director of the Center for Organizational and Human Resource Effectiveness (COHRE) and Professor of Psychology at Middle Tennessee State University (MTSU). Dr. Moffett received his PhD in Industrial-Organizational (I-O) Psychology from Auburn University in 1996. Dr. Moffett has over 30 years of experience as a consultant to private and public sector organizations, and higher education organizations. Dr. Moffett's areas of consulting expertise include leadership-management training and development, organizational diagnosis and development, survey design and development, group facilitation, and training development and evaluation. While at MTSU, Dr. Moffett has performed many roles. He has served as the internship coordinator for the I-O psychology graduate program for more than 10 years. Dr. Moffett helped found COHRE and served as the first Director. Dr. Moffett is a member of the Society for Industrial and Organizational Psychology and the Society for Human Resource Management.

Morrie Mullins is a Professor of Industrial-Organizational Psychology at Xavier University's MA I-O program in Cincinnati, Ohio. He has chaired over 60 master's theses to completion and served as a committee member on many more theses and dissertations. He received his PhD in I-O from Michigan State University in 2000 and taught at Virginia Tech and Bowling Green State University prior to coming to Xavier. In addition to his work as a faculty member, he has chaired the Xavier University Institutional Review Board for the past 10 years. His research interests center around selection and assessment, as well as issues related to humanitarian work psychology and volunteerism. When he isn't reading or writing about I-O, he's probably reading fiction, or writing his own fiction.

Yoshie Nakai is an Associate Professor of Industrial-Organizational Psychology at Eastern Kentucky University. She earned her PhD in Industrial/Gerontological Psychology from the University of Akron. She is certified through the Society for Human Resource Management as a Senior Certified Professional. Her research focuses on career development and aging at work. Yoshie is also the Director of the Center for Applied Psychology and Workforce Development at Eastern Kentucky University. In this role, she consults with a variety of organizations and coordinates undergraduate and graduate student practicum experience.

Daniel A. Sachau received a PhD in Social Psychology from the University of Utah. He is a Professor of Psychology in the Industrial-Organizational Psychology Graduate Program at Minnesota State University and is the Director of the Organizational Effectiveness Research Group (OERG) at MSU. The OERG provides research and consulting services to public and private organizations. Dan's research interests are focused on employee motivation, job attitudes, and sports psychology. Dan served as the Director of the I-O Graduate Program for over 20 years and was the recipient of the 2010

Society of Industrial-Organizational Psychology Distinguished Teaching Contributions Award.

Adriane M. F. Sanders is an Associate Professor of Psychological Science and Program Director of the Master of Science in Industrial-Organizational Psychology program at Austin Peay State University. She enjoys teaching "on ground" and online at the undergraduate and master's level. Adriane has served on various applied projects related to higher education, highway safety, health care, local business, and the U.S. Navy, and was previously affiliated with the Center for Research on Women at the University of Memphis. Her research interests include work–life interaction (particularly in academia), quality of (work) life, stress, graduate training, pedagogy in the psychological discipline, and corporate environmental sustainability. She promotes the use of empirical research to empower women (and all gender identities) to make informed decisions about their work life, wellbeing, health, and safety.

Kimberly T. Schneider is an Associate Professor of Psychology and Coordinator of the Master's Program in Industrial-Organizational and Social Psychology at Illinois State University. As part of the required thesis component for the program, she has supervised more than 50 thesis students since 2001. Prior to joining the faculty at Illinois State University, she coordinated the MA and PhD programs in Organizational Psychology at the University of Texas at El Paso and served on over 20 thesis and dissertation committees. Dr. Schneider received her PhD in I-O Psychology from the University of Illinois at Urbana-Champaign in 1996. Her research interests are related to employee attitudes and wellbeing, with a focus on workplace harassment and coping.

Linda Rhoades Shanock is a Professor of Psychology at UNC Charlotte and a nationally board-certified reflexologist. She earned her PhD from the University of Delaware in Social Psychology. Linda has published over 35 articles and has been named one of the top 100 most cited scholars in the field of management. Throughout her career she has focused her research on employee wellbeing, particularly research involving perceived organizational support (POS) because there are a host of positive outcomes when one feels valued and cared about by one's work organization. She plans to continue to work in the employee wellbeing area with future research focusing on the physical and emotional wellbeing that comes from working for a supportive organization and on intervention studies to improve employee wellness. She is an actively practicing reflexologist, regularly seeing clients who report stress reduction from the sessions.

Elizabeth L. Shoenfelt, University Distinguished Professor in the Department of Psychological Sciences at Western Kentucky University, has directed the WKU Industrial-Organizational Psychology Graduate Program for 25+ years. She received her PhD in 1983 from LSU in I-O Psychology with minors in Sport Psychology and Statistics. She is a licensed I-O Psychologist, a Certified Mental Performance Consultant®, a Fellow of the Society for Industrial and Organizational Psychology and the Association for Applied Sport Psychology, and a member of the United States Olympic & Paralympic Committee's Sport Psychology and Mental Skills Registry. In 2013, she received the SIOP Distinguished Teaching Contributions Award. She teaches graduate courses in I-O and directs thesis research and I-O internships. She has 35+ years of consulting experience in business, industry, government, education, and sports. Her I-O work focuses on selection, EEO issues, organizational justice in team settings, performance management, and pedagogical issues. In sports, she works with teams and individually with coaches and athletes at the intercollegiate, Olympic, and professional levels.

Kenneth S. Shultz is a Professor of Psychology in the Department of Psychology at California State University, San Bernardino. His MA and PhD degrees are in Industrial and Organizational (I-O) Psychology from Wayne State University in Detroit, Michigan. He also completed postdoctoral work in social gerontology at the Andrus Gerontology Center at the University of Southern California. Professor Shultz teaches classes in I-O psychology, research methods, psychological testing, and statistics at both the undergraduate and graduate level. He is the current Director of the Master of Science in I-O Psychology program at CSUSB. He has published 55 peer-reviewed articles in journals such as the *American Psychologist, Journal of Management, Journal of Applied Psychology, Journal of Business and Psychology, Journal of Occupational Health Psychology,* and *Work, Employment, and Society.* He was the recipient of the 2014–2015 John M. Pfau Outstanding Professor Award at CSUSB.

Nancy J. Stone, Professor of Psychological Sciences at Missouri University of Science and Technology, founded the Missouri S&T I-O master's program.

She received her PhD with an emphasis in I-O Psychology from Texas Tech in 1987. For 30+ years she has been a leader in I-O pedagogy, having served on the SIOP Education and Training Committee, regularly presented at the SIOP conference, and published numerous articles related to the training and teaching of I-O at the undergraduate and master's levels. At Missouri S&T, she has served as a Faculty Fellow, Department Head, and Special Assistant to the Provost for Analytics, Planning, and Assessment; she served as a Faculty Fellow for NASA and the Air Force. In addition to SIOP membership, she is an active member of the Human Factors and Ergonomics Society and is the lead author on the 2018 textbook *Introduction to Human Factors: Applying Psychology to Design.*

1

An Introduction to
Industrial-Organizational Psychology

Elizabeth L. Shoenfelt, Rosemary Hays-Thomas,
and Laura Koppes Bryan

Industrial-organizational (I-O) psychology likely touches the lives of virtually everyone who works in an organization. Nonetheless, most in the general public, including faculty in departments without I-O programs, are not aware of I-O psychology and what the discipline encompasses (ABC News, 2014; Gasser, Butler, Waddilove, & Tan, 2004; Gasser, Whitsett, Mosley, Sullivan, Rogers, & Tan, 1998; Lowe, 1997; Ryan, 2003), or the positive impact it has on work and wellbeing (Campion, 1996). One of the primary objectives for this book is to address this lack of familiarity by explaining the content and practice of I-O psychology, including various aspects of the graduate training needed to become an I-O psychologist. This will in turn facilitate the advisement of young adults in careers in I-O psychology. In addition, this book focuses on education and training in I-O psychology at the master's level as distinct from doctoral preparation. In this volume, we address the application process, curriculum issues, applied experiences, and issues for faculty. In doing so we provide best practices for those who teach I-O psychology at the master's level.

We begin this chapter with a brief description of the discipline of I-O psychology, detailing activities and objectives of both the industrial and the organizational foci. This is followed by a discussion of I-O graduate training and what distinguishes master's training from doctoral training. We then address challenges facing I-O master's programs and the recent actions by the Society for Industrial and Organizational Psychology (SIOP) and the American Psychological Association (APA) with respect to I-O master's programs. We conclude with a brief preview of the other six chapters in this volume.

Elizabeth L. Shoenfelt, Rosemary Hays-Thomas, and Laura Koppes Bryan, *An Introduction to Industrial-Organizational Psychology* In: *Mastering Industrial-Organizational Psychology.* Edited by: Elizabeth L. Shoenfelt, Oxford University Press (2020). © Society for Industrial and Organizational Psychology. DOI: 10.1093/oso/9780190071141.003.0001.

Brief Introduction to I-O Psychology

SIOP, the national organization for I-O psychologists, defines I-O psychology as the scientific study of the workplace. I-O psychologists apply the knowledge, principles, and scientific methods of psychology to issues of critical relevance to business, including talent management, coaching, assessment, selection, training, organizational development, motivation, leadership, and performance (SIOP, 2019a). Specifically, I-O psychologists use science and practice to assist organizations and the people in those organizations to achieve maximum work effectiveness. I-O psychologists work in human resource (HR) management, talent acquisition and management, organization development, consulting, people analytics, and many other organizational units. Job titles for master's-level I-O psychologists include assessment manager, client relations manager, compensation and benefits analyst, compliance coordinator, continuous improvement specialist, consultant, data analytics specialist, diversity and inclusion consultant, employee engagement specialist, environmental health and safety manager, examination analyst, global organizational survey director, human resources information systems consultant, HR manager/specialist/coordinator, institutional research and effectiveness analyst, instructional systems designer/analyst, leadership development advisor, labor relations manager, marketing analyst, organization development consultant/specialist, people development manager, personnel analyst, personnel research analyst, program manager, project manager, selection and assessment consulting analyst, survey statistician, talent acquisition specialist, training and development coordinator, quality assurance, workforce analytics, and, occasionally, I-O psychologist—to name just a few. This variety of work settings and job titles is one of the reasons many do not realize the prevalence of I-O psychologists in the workforce. Accordingly, we now will describe in more detail the content of I-O psychology beginning with the industrial/personnel focus followed by the organizational focus.

To ensure individuals *can* perform the job effectively, the practice of personnel psychology frequently begins with a job analysis that systematically identifies the essential work requirements of a job (e.g., tasks, equipment, context) as well as the knowledge, skills, abilities, and other attributes (KSAOs) needed by the individual(s) who will perform the work. The information from the job analysis becomes the foundation for many I-O practices. The I-O psychologist may observe and/or interview workers and review job descriptions as a first step, but a job analysis typically also includes systematic collection of data about the job from subject matter experts. Subject matter experts, who may be job incumbents, supervisors, or others familiar with the job, may answer job analysis questionnaires addressing job behaviors and responsibilities. Data from these questionnaires provide information about the tasks performed on the job, the equipment used to perform the job, and work conditions such as hazardous or demanding situations or a team context. Questionnaires addressing worker requirements identify specific KSAOs necessary for effective job performance. KSAOs may include specific educational or experiential requirements, cognitive or physical abilities, or personality traits such as conscientiousness. Job analysis data may be collected for a variety of purposes, including developing selection systems, performance management systems, or training programs. The information collected in the job analysis will vary depending on the purpose for which the job analysis was conducted. Frequently, the job analysis results in a job description summarizing the job analysis information.

Selection programs ensure that organizations hire or promote the applicants who are most capable of performing well in the job. Job analysis provides the foundation for developing selection programs by identifying the KSAOs needed to perform the job. I-O psychologists are trained to develop and validate tests and other selection instruments that measure these KSAOs; the tests are then used to identify job applicants who have the ability to perform the job effectively. Selection programs typically include multiple assessments such as application blanks, interviews, and tests specifically designed to assess the KSAOs identified in the job analysis. Tests may include written knowledge tests, physical abilities tests, personality tests, or other tests assessing specific skills needed for the job. An important role of I-O psychologists is to validate selection tests to ensure that they reliably and accurately measure the required job skills and that test performance is related to job performance—that is, those who perform well on the test also perform well on the job. Establishing test validity enables organizations to use these tests to select the best applicants for the job.

Once workers are on the job, organizations must manage their performance. Information from the job analysis can be used to develop performance management systems to guide and evaluate employee performance. Job analysis information is used to identify what aspects of job performance should be measured and the level of performance that meets the standards for acceptable performance. Based on this information, I-O psychologists develop performance appraisal systems that outline specific expectations for job performance and provide a format for evaluating performance and mechanisms for giving performance feedback. If properly implemented, the performance management system clarifies what is to be done on the job and ensures workers who are performing well are recognized and rewarded for their good performance. Any workers not performing up to standard are provided feedback and an opportunity to improve their performance. Performance management systems also provide the basis for career development and for identifying training needs.

Because organizations cannot always hire employees with all requisite skills and because some skills become obsolete or new skill demands arise, I-O psychologists develop training programs. Job analysis data on both the task and KSAOs are essential to developing and evaluating training programs. Based on a training needs analysis at the organizational, job, and individual level, I-O psychologists identify the training objectives for the organization, the skills that must be trained for particular jobs, and the employees who need training. Some training programs are mandated by law, for example sexual harassment training or safety training. I-O psychologists rely on their expertise in learning theory and performance science to design training programs that use appropriate training methods (e.g., computer simulations, classroom learning, on-the-job training) to teach the KSAOs identified in the needs analysis. I-O psychologists also evaluate training programs to ensure the KSAOs actually were learned in the training and that this learning transferred to the job. They may also conduct return-on-investment evaluations to ensure the training programs result in increased productivity for the organization.

Each of these personnel practices must be conducted within the boundaries of Equal Employment Opportunity laws and guidelines, such as Title VII of the Civil Rights Act, the Americans with Disabilities Act, the Age Discrimination in Employment Act, the Equal Pay Act, the Uniform Guidelines for Employee Selection Practices, and other labor laws. Accordingly, I-O psychologists must be well versed in Equal Employment Opportunity law. Indeed, I-O psychologists play important roles when these laws are constructed by Congress and tried in courts by testifying, consulting, writing amicus briefs, and serving as expert witnesses to ensure that laws are fair and are consistent with best personnel practices. The laws require that personnel decisions are based on job-related characteristics and job performance rather than class characteristics protected by law such as race, sex, age, or disability. Personnel practices of I-O psychologists are likewise designed to ensure fair policies and procedures. These practices all fall within the "industrial" focus of I-O psychology (also referred to as personnel psychology) and help to ensure the individual is capable of performing the job.

We move now to the other major area of I-O psychology, the "organizational" focus, which helps to ensure the individual *will* perform the job and remain engaged and satisfied. Organizational psychologists work at the individual, group/team, and organizational level. At the macro level, I-O psychologists apply organizational theory to find the optimal design for organizations and units within organizations. In rapidly changing environments, the most effective design may be an organization with small units that have autonomy to respond quickly to dynamic changes in products, services, technology, and clients. In more stable environments where the services, products, and processes are well established, organizational units may be larger, with more individuals working under a given manager or supervisor. I-O psychologists specializing in organization development assist organizations in planned, data-based efforts, managed from the top, to grow and develop in response to the ever-changing demands of the work environment, including the global economy, technology, and client products and services.

At the group level, organizational psychologists work with teams, group dynamics, and leaders to ensure performance effectiveness. I-O psychologists who study leadership derive principles for effective leader behavior to address task/performance issues, interpersonal issues, and the interaction of leaders and followers. Leadership is a complex phenomenon and is rarely explained by a single theory. Accordingly, the study of leadership involves evaluating different theories and principles and determining their effectiveness in a variety of situations. I-O psychologists also work with teams to improve team dynamics. When team members have highly differentiated and nonredundant skills, clearly delineating individual roles on a team is critical as the performance of a single team member can have an important impact on the performance of the entire team. Team building can include identifying team values and team objectives and understanding interpersonal dynamics. A number of I-O psychologists are involved in researching team dynamics for NASA's mission to Mars, where the space crew will be confined together in a small space for as long as 240 days (e.g., Hewer & Sleek, 2018; Salas, Tannenbaum, Kozlowski, Miller, Mathieu, & Vessey, 2015).

At the individual level, I-O psychologists address issues such as motivation and attitudes, including job satisfaction, commitment, and perceptions of fairness. As with leadership, motivation is a complex construct and a number of theories attempt to explain why we direct our efforts toward and persist in the pursuit of some activities and not others. For example, setting specific, challenging goals that are understood, accepted, and paired with feedback is a straightforward mechanism for increasing performance in relation to those goals. Reinforcement theory explains motivation in terms of the consequences of our actions: We are more likely to continue activities that result in positive outcomes. Instrumentality theory brings in a cognitive component and suggests that we evaluate whether we expect our efforts to result in a given performance, whether that performance will lead to given outcomes, and how much we value those outcomes. Behavior that is motivated by outcomes is said to be extrinsically motivated and stands in contrast to intrinsically motivated behavior that we engage in because it is inherently rewarding to do so. Both extrinsic motivation (e.g., pay, praise, prestige) and intrinsic motivation (e.g., altruistic behavior, hobbies) are effective ways to influence behavior. However, intrinsic motivation tends to be longer lasting and to promote more commitment and persistence in working toward task accomplishment than does extrinsic motivation. Most behavior is multiply determined; that is, a number of different forces are likely to drive our behavior at any given time. Typically, more than one theory of motivation is needed to explain complex performance.

I-O psychologists recognize the important role of attitudes such as job satisfaction, commitment, and perceptions of fairness; they study the antecedents and consequences of these attitudes. Job satisfaction and commitment have similar antecedents and consequences such that some I-O psychologists believe the two constructs are highly related. *Organizational justice* is the term used to describe perceptions of fairness in the workplace. Typically, I-O psychologists speak in terms of procedural (how decisions are made), distributive (how resources are allocated among employees), and interactional (interpersonal aspects) justice. Although all three components of justice are important, if employees believe the procedure used to allocate resources is fair and they have had a voice in the decision, this can override a negative perception of the distribution of outcomes. For example, if office space is assigned based on merit, even those with a smaller office are likely to perceive it as a fair decision. Negative attitudes such as dissatisfaction, a lack of commitment, or a perceived lack of fairness can lead to negative outcomes such as psychological withdrawal, turnover, or job stress. Accordingly, it is important for organizations to create a work environment that promotes positive attitudes.

In summary, it is evident that with both the industrial and organizational foci of I-O psychology, science and practice are used to ensure people in organizations can and will perform their jobs effectively. Next we discuss the graduate training needed to become an I-O psychologist.

I-O Master's Training

Training in I-O psychology typically involves earning a graduate degree, either a master's degree or a doctorate (PhD). A limited number of universities offer an undergraduate major or concentration in I-O psychology (Bott, Stuhlmacher, & Powaser, 2006). Those with an undergraduate degree in I-O are prepared to go directly into entry-level HR management positions. Generally, a master's degree requires two years of study after completing a bachelor's degree and often some additional experience (e.g., thesis or internship). Master's graduates are prepared for more responsible HR jobs or for employment in some consulting or research contexts. A doctorate can require between four and seven years of postgraduate work. Doctoral graduates usually complete a dissertation and some complete an internship as well. They are qualified for jobs as faculty in higher education, researchers, or consultants and may be licensed in states where this credential is available to I-O psychologists. As noted in the beginning of this chapter, this book focuses on graduate training at the master's level.

According to the SIOP *Guidelines for Education and Training in Industrial-Organizational Psychology* (SIOP, 2016), master's and doctoral I-O graduate students receive training in many of the same competencies, although there is a difference in the breadth and depth of training. Doctoral students gain more knowledge of theory while master's students tend to have a more applied orientation. As noted, the timeframe for a terminal master's program is typically half the time of a doctoral program. Master's programs train scientist-practitioners within a truncated, two-year timeframe. Within these two years, a master's student can gain a comprehensive education that covers the key competencies. Thus, it is possible to train scientist-practitioners at the master's level (Kottke, Shoenfelt, & Stone, 2014; cf. Erffmeyer & Mendel, 1990; Kottke, 1994; Shultz & Kottke, 1997; Trahan & McAllister, 2002).

Master's-level I-O psychology graduate programs have grown exponentially over the past several decades. In 1983, there were fewer than 15 I-O master's programs (E. L. Shoenfelt, personal communication, September

1983). In 1993, Lowe reported 55 I-O master's programs. In January 2019, SIOP listed 185 I-O master's programs on its website. Most of these programs are standalone degree programs not affiliated with a doctoral program (Koppes, 1991b; SIOP, 2019a). Master's programs outnumber doctoral programs on the SIOP graduate training website (SIOP, 2019a), and master's programs produce far more graduates than do doctoral programs. Estimates from the SIOP website (2019a) indicate that there are 3,856 graduate students currently enrolled in I-O master's programs, more than the estimated 3,244 students currently enrolled in doctoral programs. Furthermore, the website estimates that close to three times as many students graduate each year from master's programs (1850) compared to doctoral programs (520). Because more master's cohorts graduate over a fixed time period, many more students will graduate with master's degrees than with doctorates within a given time period.

In a 2014 report by the U.S. Bureau of Labor Statistics, I-O psychology was identified as the occupation with the highest projected growth rate from 2012 to 2022, with a reported median salary of $83,580 (ABC News, 2014). In May 2018, the U.S. Bureau of Labor Statistics continued to identify I-O psychology as a top job with a median income of $97,260 (U.S. Bureau of Labor Statistics, 2019). Clearly, I-O psychologists and, particularly master's-level I-O psychologists, have a bright future.

Next, we discuss characteristics of and challenges facing I-O master's programs, and the recent SIOP and APA attention to I-O master's programs. Finally, we preview the remaining six chapters in this book and mention a second SIOP Professional Practice Series book on careers for I-O master's-level psychologists.

Master's I-O Psychologists in Particular

Earlier we mentioned that the prevalence of I-O psychologists in organizations is hidden because of the variety of their work settings and job titles. For master's I-O psychologists, additional factors prevent recognition of their numbers and the variety and scope of their work. These factors arise both between psychology and other fields, and within the field of psychology itself.

First, many master's I-O practitioners work in fields and with job titles that also include a range of master's graduates in other areas. For example, various types of work in HR may be performed by those with degrees in HR itself, HR management, business, management, adult education, or other fields. Researchers or consultants may have degrees in areas such as statistics, organization development, or business administration.

Second, many master's-degree programs in I-O are actually titled as degrees in "psychology" rather than I-O psychology. This nomenclature usually occurs for bureaucratic, political, or legal reasons having to do with the mandate of the degree-granting institution rather than the specific content of the program. Accordingly, in many psychology graduate programs, students in I-O, clinical/counseling, or general/research psychology all earn a master's degree in psychology.

Regardless of the title, a degree in I-O psychology differs greatly from the better-known and widely earned master of business administration (MBA) degree. The MBA curriculum focuses on general business and management functions and may include specific courses in accounting, finance, marketing, organizational behavior, or business law (Kagan, 2019). In contrast, typical coursework in I-O psychology covers the areas described earlier, such as job analysis, performance appraisal and management, employment law, measurement and statistics, research design, organization development, leadership, and team processes, to name a few. Students in an applied I-O master's program not only learn *about* these things, but they also typically *apply* this information in course projects, practica, and/or internships.

Within the field of psychology, including I-O psychology, a variety of factors affect the recognition of the size and role of the master's I-O psychology workforce. First, across many academic fields focused on doctoral preparation, the role of the master's degree has been unclear (e.g., American Historical Association, 2005). Contemporary psychology is no different. Many doctoral institutions offer a master's degree as part of a doctoral program. In these institutions, the master's is considered not a "terminal" degree but instead a milestone in progress toward the doctorate. The "consolation prize" view of the master's degree arose because the master's was sometimes awarded to students who were counseled to discontinue further study toward a doctoral degree. Faculty of many psychology departments are only familiar with this model and have no experience with, or information about, curricula that are carefully designed to prepare graduates for employment at the master's level.

Furthermore, master's degrees embedded in doctoral programs are generally not applied degrees but instead preparation for the advanced scholarship and research required of doctoral graduates. In addition, a few institutions offer a curriculum that is a "research-oriented master's program designed specifically to prepare students for doctoral work" (Wake Forest University, 2012). Thus, it is not surprising that a lack of clarity exists about the specific role of an applied master's program designed to prepare graduates for meaningful employment beyond the entry level.

Within psychology, a second factor has added to confusion and skepticism about the I-O psychology master's degree (Lowe, 1993; Lowe Hays-Thomas, 2000). For many years, the politics of the field of psychology, particularly within the APA, have been dominated by clinical psychologists involved in providing mental health services. In the attempt to demonstrate status and professionalism competitive with those of psychiatry and other medical fields, and in the context of provision of mental health services by the Veterans Administration to veterans of World War II, a doctoral standard was adopted within psychology in state licensure requirements for independent practice (Humphreys, 1996). Licensure laws often restrict both the *title* of psychologist and the practice of work in the field. Frequently in psychology, only those who are licensed (at the doctoral level) can legally call themselves "psychologists." In later years, doctoral psychologists sought to distinguish themselves from other master's-level mental health providers in social work (master of social work degree), counseling, mental health counseling, and other fields. The master's degree in psychology, even outside the clinical or mental health areas, fell victim to this dynamic and has been systematically excluded from consideration even in the context of educational programming. For example, the APA's Education Directorate offers resources and attention for postdoctoral, doctoral, undergraduate, and precollege education as well as continuing education—but not about master's-level education (APA, 2019).

Within the I-O community, oriented as the field is toward practice and research within organizations, the doctoral criterion has seemed less relevant. The competition for providing services to business and industry comes from providers with varied educational backgrounds at different degree levels. As described in a later section, master's students, graduates, and programs have been incorporated into national programming such as the SIOP annual conference. Yet because of the factors cited in the past few paragraphs, some misunderstanding and lack of information about the preparation and work of master's-prepared I-O psychologists continues. Perhaps because of SIOP's existence as a division of APA (although with its own governance), until recently SIOP maintained a separate membership category for master's graduates.

In 1991, several SIOP members involved with master's education participated in a symposium at the sixth annual SIOP conference titled *Industrial and Organizational Psychology Master's Level Training: Reality in Search of Legitimacy* (Koppes, 1991a). At that time, it was evident to these participants that there was a long history of master's education in I-O psychology, but master's programs were yet to be recognized as a legitimate approach to preparing researchers and practitioners. For many years, SIOP's membership mirrored the opinions of APA's members that the doctorate was the only legitimate degree in psychology; however, more recently SIOP's executive committees have been open to implementing policies and strategies that recognize the value and importance of preparing master's graduates for the research and practice of I-O psychology. For example, education and training guidelines were established for master's programs and have been revised. The 2016 revision of the *Guidelines for Education and Training in Industrial-Organizational Psychology* (SIOP, 2016) includes a section on the difference between master's and doctoral education but recommends the same General Knowledge and Skills and Core I-O Content competencies for both master's and doctoral training. Master's program faculty and students have always been welcomed to the SIOP annual conferences, and every year there are program sessions specifically targeted to master's program faculty and graduate students (e.g., Lowe, Kottke, & Siegfried, 1996; Shoenfelt, Fotouhi, Kedenburg, Palmer, Seibert, & Walker, 2017; Simerson, Seigfried, Lowe, Koppes, & Farr, 1993; Stone, Shoenfelt, Huffcut, Morganson, & Frame, 2018; Stone, Shoenfelt, Morganson, Moffett, & Van Hein, 2017).

I-O master's degree holders can join SIOP as associate members with all the member benefits except voting rights. Recently, SIOP has further recognized master's education as a legitimate approach to preparing researchers and practitioners. For example, a special task force proposed a pathway for associate members who have fulfilled additional requirements to become full members with voting rights; this pathway was approved and now is SIOP policy and practice (SIOP, 2019b). This book, as a text in SIOP's Professional Practice series, is another example of clear evidence that SIOP is giving serious attention to master's programs, faculty, and graduates.

Unfortunately, APA does not have consensus on the value of master's education generally and continues to ignore master's-level preparation of psychologists in I-O specifically. As recently as 2018, a special section was published in *Professional Psychology: Research and Practice* that focused on master's training in psychological practice. The articles stemmed from a 2016 Master's Summit in which this question was asked: "Should APA embrace the training of psychological practitioners at the master's level?" (p. 299; Campbell, Dailey, Worrell, & Brown, 2018). The opening article of the special section concluded with the following:

> Now, the practice community is split by those who affiliate with health or medical systems and see the merits of master's-level practitioners in their hierarchy and those who identify as independent practitioners and still question the compatibility of master's and doctoral psychological practitioners in the market place together. The education community sees the potential in training and development of the master's-level professional. (Campbell, Dailey, Worrell, & Brown, 2018, p. 304)

The focus was clearly on clinical and counseling psychology. To date, we are not aware of any efforts by APA to recognize master's education in I-O psychology. The impact of APA's lack of attention to I-O master's education is unknown but is likely to be minimal except as it pertains to licensure in some states when licensure is relevant. SIOP is the primary professional affiliate of most I-O psychologists, many of whom do not belong to APA. Likely of greater importance is SIOP's recent increased efforts to include and support master's-level I-O programs and practitioners.

Conclusion

The future looks bright for I-O master's programs and their graduates. I-O master's programs are receiving increased attention and support from SIOP. The job market for I-O psychologists is strong and is predicted to remain so for at least the next decade (U.S. Bureau of Labor Statistics, 2019). This volume provides best practices for training master's-level I-O psychologists. The remaining six chapters offer advice about applying to graduate school, including considerations for selecting a master's program; a detailed review of the SIOP *Guidelines for Education and Training in Industrial-Organizational Psychology* (SIOP, 2016) and various methods for teaching the identified competencies; guidance on implementing important applied experiences such as course projects, practica, and internships; the pros and cons of a thesis requirement; issues faced by faculty in I-O master's programs, including strategies for balancing teaching, service, and research; and, finally, advice for developing and maintaining an on-campus I-O consulting entity.

The best practices presented in this volume, offered by faculty from top-ranked I-O master's programs (Acikgoz et al., 2018; Vodanovich, Morganson, & Kass, 2018), should be of interest to faculty teaching in master's I-O programs and other teaching-intensive institutions who can learn best practices in training I-O graduate students at the master's level. The book should be very useful to I-O faculty and non-I-O psychology faculty in advising undergraduates on career options in psychology, specifically as an I-O master's practitioner. Undergraduates considering a career in I-O psychology will find the content of this book to be valuable in determining whether I-O psychology is a good career fit for them and in evaluating I-O master's programs to find one that provides the training to meet their career interests. The sister SIOP Professional Practice Series volume to this book, *Mastering the Job Market: Career Issues for Master's-Level Industrial-Organizational Psychologists* (Shoenfelt, in press), contains important information about careers, based on a nationwide study of I-O master's graduates and insights from I-O master's faculty from some of the strongest I-O master's programs (Acikgoz et al., 2018; Vodanovich, Morganson, & Kass, 2018).

References

ABC News. (2014). https://abcnews.go.com/Business/americas-20-fastest-growing-jobs-surprise/story?id=22364716

Acikgoz, Y., Huelsman, T. J., Swets J. L., Dixon, A. R., Jeffer, S. N., Olsen, D. R., & Ross, A. (2018). The cream of the crop: Student and alumni perceptions of I-O psychology master's degree program quality. *The Industrial-Organizational Psychologist*, *55*(4). http://my.siop.org/tip/jan18/editor/ArtMID/13745/ArticleID/334/The-Cream-of-the-Crop-Student-and-Alumni-Perceptions-of-I-O-Psychology-Masters-Degree-Program-Quality

American Historical Association. (2005). Retrieving the master's degree from the dustbin of history. https://www.historians.org/about-aha-and-membership/aha-history-and-archives/historical-archives/retrieving-the-master's-degree-from-the-dustbin-of-history

American Psychological Association. (2019). Education and training resource documents. https://www.apa.org/ed/resources/index

Bott, J. P., Stuhlmacher, A. F., & Powaser, P. R. (2006). The invisible pipeline: I-O at the undergraduate level. *The Industrial-Organizational Psychologist, 44*(2), 123–127. https://doi.org/10.1037/e579112011-018

Campbell, L. F., Dailey, A. T., Worrell, F. C., & Brown, R. T. (2018). Master's level practice: Introduction, history, and current status. *Professional Psychology: Research and Practice, 49*(5–6), 299–305. doi:10.1037/pro0000202

Campion, M. (1996). Why I am proud to be an I-O psychologist. *The Industrial-Organizational Psychologist, 34*(1), 27–29. https://doi.org/10.1037/e577102011-004

Erffmeyer, E. S., & Mendel, R. M. (1990). Master's level training in industrial/organizational psychology: A case study of the perceived relevance of graduate training. *Professional Psychology: Research and Practice, 21*(5), 405. doi:10.1037/0735-7028.21.5.405

Gasser, M., Butler, A., Waddilove, L., & Tan, R. (2004). Defining the profession of industrial-organizational psychology. *The Industrial-Organizational Psychologist, 42*(2), 15–20. https://doi.org/10.1037/e578782011-002

Gasser, M., Whitsett, D., Mosley, N., Sullivan, K., Rogers, T., & Tan, R. (1998). I-O psychology: What's your line? *The Industrial-Organizational Psychologist, 35*(4). https://doi.org/10.1037/e577062011-013

Hewer, M., & Sleek, S. (2018, November). Teams in space: It isn't just rocket science. *Association for Psychological Science Observer.* https://www.psychologicalscience.org/observer/teams-in-space-it-isnt-just-rocket-science

Humphreys, K. (1996). Clinical psychologists as psychotherapists: History, future, and alternatives. *American Psychologist, 51,* 190–197. https://doi.org/10.1037/0003-066X.51.3.190

Kagan, J. (2019, April 13). Master of Business Administration. https://www.investopedia.com/terms/m/mba.asp

Koppes, L. L. (Chair). (1991a, April). *Industrial and organizational psychology master's level training: Reality in search of legitimacy.* Symposium conducted at the 6th Annual Conference of the Society for Industrial and Organizational Psychology, Inc., St. Louis, MO.

Koppes, L. L. (1991b). I-O psychology master's level training: Reality and legitimacy in search of recognition. *The Industrial-Organizational Psychologist, 29*(2), 59–67. https://doi.org/10.1037/e579482009-010

Kottke, J. L. (1994, August). Training scientist-practitioners at the master's degree level. In K. S. Shultz (Chair & Discussant), *Undergraduate and graduate education in I/O psychology: What next?* Symposium conducted at the annual conference of the American Psychological Association Meeting, Los Angeles, CA.

Kottke, J. L., Shoenfelt, E. L., & Stone, N. J. (2014). Educating industrial-organizational psychologists: Lessons learned from master's programs. *Industrial and Organizational Psychology, 7,* 26–31. https://doi.org/10.1111/iops.12099

Lowe, R. H. (1993). Master's programs in industrial-organizational psychology: Current status and a call for action. *Professional Psychology: Research and Practice, 24,* 27–34. https://doi.org/10.1037/0735-7028.24.1.27

Lowe, R. H. (1997). Employment realities and possibilities for master's level psychological personnel. *Journal of Psychological Practice, 3*(1), 47–54.

Lowe, R. H., Kottke, J. L., & Siegfried, W. D., Jr. (1996, April). *Where the guidelines stop: Implementing a master's curriculum in I/O psychology.* Roundtable presented at 11th Annual Meeting of the Society for Industrial and Organizational Psychology, San Diego, CA.

Lowe Hays-Thomas, R. (2000). The silent conversation: Talking about the master's degree. *Professional Psychology: Research and Practice, 31,* 339–345. doi:10.1037//0735-7028.31.3.339

Ryan, A. M. (2003). Defining ourselves: I-O psychology's identity quest. *The Industrial-Organizational Psychologist, 41*(1), 21–33. https://doi.org/10.1037/e578792011-002

Salas, E., Tannenbaum, S. I., Kozlowski, S. W., Miller, C. A., Mathieu, J. E., & Vessey, W. B. (2015). Teams in space exploration: A new frontier for the science of team effectiveness. *Current Directions in Psychological Science, 24,* 200–207. doi:10.1177/0963721414566448

Shoenfelt, E. L. (Ed.). (in press). *Mastering the job market: Career issues for master's-level industrial-organizational psychologists.* New York: Oxford University Press.

Shoenfelt, E. L., Fotouhi, C. H., Kedenburg, G. L., Palmer, L., Seibert, J., & Walker, S. A. (2017, April). "Mastering" the job market: Advice from master's level professionals. Presented at the Annual Conference of the Society for Industrial & Organizational Psychology, Orlando, FL.

Shultz, K. S., & Kottke, J. L. (1997). The master's thesis in applied psychology training. *Teaching of Psychology, 23,* 166–168. https://doi.org/10.1177/009862839602300307

Simerson, G. R., Seigfried, W. D., Lowe, R. H., Koppes, L. L., & Farr, J. L. (1993, April). *Master's level industrial and organizational training: Recent developments and implications for SIOP.* Roundtable discussion conducted at the 8th Annual Conference of the Society for Industrial and Organizational Psychology, Inc., San Francisco, CA.

Society for Industrial and Organizational Psychology, Inc. (2016). *Guidelines for education and training in industrial-organizational psychology.* Bowling Green, OH: Author. https://www.siop.org/Events-Education/Graduate-Training-Program/Guidelines-for-Education-and-Training

Society for Industrial and Organizational Psychology, Inc. (2019a). http://siop.org/GTP/

Society for Industrial and Organizational Psychology, Inc. (2019b). https://www.siop.org/Membership/Associate-to-Member

Stone, N. J., Shoenfelt, E. L., Huffcut, A. I., Morganson, V. J., & Frame, M. C. (2018, April). Maintaining research and consulting activities in teaching intensive institutions. Presented at the Annual Conference of the Society for Industrial and Organizational Psychology, Chicago, IL.

Stone, N. J., Shoenfelt, E. L., Morganson, V. J., Moffett, R. G., & Van Hein, J. L. (2017, April). Developing employability with master's and undergraduate internships. Presented at the Annual Conference of the Society for Industrial and Organizational Psychology, Orlando, FL.

Trahan, W. A., & McAllister, H. A. (2002). Master's level training in industrial/organizational psychology: Does it meet the SIOP Guidelines? *Journal of Business and Psychology, 16*(3), 457–465. https://doi.org/10.1023/A:1012881209342

U.S. Bureau of Labor Statistics. (2019, May). https://www.bls.gov/oes/current/oes193032.htm

Vodanovich, S. J., Morganson, V. J., & Kass, S. J. (2018) Ranking I-O master's programs using objective data from I-O coordinators. *The Industrial-Organizational Psychologist*, 55(4). http://my.siop.org/tip/jan18/editor/ArtMID/13745/ArticleID/333/Ranking-I-O-Masters-Programs-Using-Objective-Data-From-I-O-Coordinators1

Wake Forest University. (2012). Wake Forest College Department of Psychology. http://psychology.wfu.edu/

2

Applying to Industrial-Organizational Master's Programs

Program Selection, Undergraduate Preparation, and Application Process

Nancy J. Stone and Adriane M. F. Sanders

A career in industrial-organizational (I-O) psychology typically requires a graduate degree at either the master's or doctoral level, although an undergraduate degree with an emphasis in I-O may lead to a career in human resources (HR). The process of applying to graduate school, as well as graduate school itself, is time consuming and can be costly. Students applying to graduate school need to find a program that best fits their career aspirations; faculty advisors can assist students with this search. It is important that students consider whether a graduate degree is necessary for their targeted career and, if so, whether they should pursue a master's or doctoral degree, as these degrees lead to different career opportunities. In addition, students should ensure I-O psychology, rather than HR or business, is the best career fit. Once a student decides to pursue a degree in I-O psychology, the student needs to understand how to prepare for and apply to I-O graduate programs. To assist students and their advisors in navigating the path to I-O graduate school, we begin with guidance on how to determine if an I-O degree at the master's level is most appropriate. We then provide steps for finding and evaluating graduate programs with special attention on delivery format. We end with a discussion on how to prepare for and apply to these programs.

Nancy J. Stone and Adriane M. F. Sanders, *Applying to Industrial-Organizational Master's Programs* In: *Mastering Industrial-Organizational Psychology*. Edited by: Elizabeth L. Shoenfelt, Oxford University Press (2020). © Society for Industrial and Organizational Psychology. DOI: 10.1093/oso/9780190071141.003.0002.

Is I-O the Right Path? If So, Which Degree Is Best?

Determining If I-O Is the Best Option

I-O psychology applies psychological science to work. Therefore, students considering a graduate degree in I-O psychology might also consider a degree in HR or business (e.g., a master of business administration [MBA] degree). Some of the Society for Human Resource Management's (2018) competencies trained in an HR master's program overlap with training in I-O, including change management, training, job analysis, performance management, recruitment and selection, and employment law. HR competencies such as HR information systems, strategic HR, employee and labor relations, and compensation and benefits typically are not covered beyond an overview in most I-O programs. An MBA program tends to focus on training in accounting, finance, management, and marketing. What makes an I-O psychology degree unique is the foundational training in the behavioral science of psychology, which enables graduates to understand complex human behavior at work. I-O psychologists are trained as scientist-practitioners; we have a better understanding of human behavior, rely on empirical data to make decisions, and tend to focus more on micro-level issues when compared to those with a business degree (Gasser, Butler, Waddilove, & Tan, 2004; Lowe, 1993). Training in I-O psychology develops skills in I-O psychology and ethics, as well as in research and statistical methods. Core competencies include individual and group behavior (e.g., attitudes, performance, individual differences, group dynamics, organizational development, and leadership and management) as well as the applied topics of personnel recruitment and selection, training, and performance management (Society for Industrial and Organizational Psychology [SIOP], 2016).

I-O Master's or Doctorate?

Once I-O is the selected field of study, the necessary level of study needs to be determined. Some individuals with a bachelor's degree in psychology might acquire jobs in HR after completing courses in I-O psychology, an internship in HR, and business or management courses. For a career in I-O psychology, a graduate degree typically is required to develop the expertise needed to independently conduct and oversee a variety of I-O activities such as job analyses, selection programs, organizational change initiatives, research, or specialized statistical analyses, to name a few. The SIOP 2016 *Guidelines for Education and Training in Industrial-Organizational Psychology* indicate that both I-O master's programs and doctoral training apply the scientist-practitioner model and develop the same core competencies. However, doctoral training provides greater breadth and depth of knowledge of the I-O competencies; master's training focuses more on applied skills and competencies (SIOP, 2016; also see Chapter 3 of this book). That is, doctoral training develops a deeper knowledge of theory and enhanced research skills; master's programs develop the applied practical skills and experiences necessary for I-O practitioners (Kottke, Shoenfelt, & Stone, 2014).

I-O master's and doctoral degrees also differ with regard to comprehensive exams and thesis or dissertation requirements. Roughly 40% of I-O psychology master's programs and all doctoral programs require a comprehensive exam (Tett, Brown, Walser, Tonidandel, & Simonet, 2013a). Similarly, 40% of I-O master's programs require a thesis, 47% have an optional thesis, and 13% do not offer a thesis, compared to business programs, where 40% have an optional thesis and 60% do not offer a thesis. All I-O doctoral programs, regardless of department, require a dissertation (Tett, Brown, & Walser, 2014).

Students interested in a doctorate may apply directly to a doctoral program, which is normally completed in five years as a full-time student. Students who complete a terminal master's degree and subsequently pursue a doctorate will likely take three to five additional years to earn their doctorate based on the doctoral faculty's evaluation and determination of what master's work will transfer as doctoral training. Many individuals with I-O doctorates work as practitioners or consultants, and a doctorate generally is required for an academic job. In contrast, a terminal I-O master's degree typically can be completed in two years of full-time study. A master's degree is a good choice for those who are considering a doctorate but want work experience first, are concerned about the long-term commitment of a doctoral program, or wish to enter the workforce more quickly as an I-O practitioner in industry, consulting, or government.

Finding Selecting an I-O Master's Program

Now the search begins for potential I-O master's programs. Using a comprehensive approach, it is important to consider interests, personal constraints, and program characteristics. Chapter 1 of this book describes the content of I-O psychology. SIOP (2016) noted the heterogeneity in content across graduate programs; thus, determining whether to pursue a career focused on industrial psychology (e.g., job analysis, employment law, personnel selection, performance management, training), organizational psychology (e.g., organizational development, leadership), or both should be an important factor in determining which graduate programs are a good fit.

Students targeting a career as a practitioner should look for programs that provide opportunities for applied experience (see Chapter 4 of this book). Nearly 60% of all I-O master's programs require internships (Tett, Brown, Walser, & Tonidandel, 2013b), and most I-O graduate students recommend completing an internship (Erffmeyer & Mendel, 1990; Shoenfelt, 2019; Shoenfelt, Stone, & Kottke, 2013). Students enrolled in a master's program that does not provide internship opportunities are encouraged to complete an internship, even if not for course credit, because internship experience has been found to increase employability (Shoenfelt et al., 2013). Students who want to work primarily in applied research or data analytics should target a program that prepares them well in research methods, data analysis, and psychometrics. Thus, students must research different programs and apply to the ones that match their interests and career aspirations.

SIOP's Graduate Training Programs (GTP) online database provides quick access to information about I-O master's programs as well as other related master's and doctoral programs. Prospective students can use this website to identify programs that match their interests and meet their needs; most programs provide links to their websites with an abundance of information (e.g., curriculum, faculty, internships). After thoroughly searching the GTP database and program website for information, students can contact program directors directly for additional information not found online. This initial contact with a graduate program can begin the process of impression formation, so it is critical to use professional language and demeanor in all correspondence.

Evaluating I-O Master's Programs

Before applying to an I-O master's program, students should evaluate whether the program is of high quality, provides appropriate training and experience, and is a good fit overall.

Accreditation

Accreditation is a rigorous process by which institutions and their programs must demonstrate quality, continuous improvement, and strategic planning, as well as programmatic and student learning outcomes (U.S. Department of Education, 2019). Neither SIOP nor the field of I-O psychology accredit graduate programs. It is wise to ensure that the university housing the I-O program under consideration is regionally accredited (easily Googled). University accreditation ensures rigorous review, analysis, and documentation that provides evidence of program quality.

Program Rankings

Students can find a variety of program rankings on the SIOP webpage (SIOP.org). For example, there are rankings based on responses from program coordinators, current students, and alumni with survey items covering objective and subjective factors, applied experiences, research productivity, and more. *The Industrial-Organizational Psychologist* recently presented two sets of extensive rankings of approximately 70 I-O master's programs (i.e., Acikgoz et al., 2018; Vodanovich, Morganson, & Kass, 2018).

Program Content

Curriculum

A review of potential I-O master's programs should include the specific courses offered. Courses should cover the core competencies identified in the *Guidelines for the Education and Training in I-O Psychology* (SIOP, 2016). As noted in the *Guidelines* (and in Chapter 3 of this book), there are multiple methods to teach these competencies. For example, a program might have a course on a competency, an applied project within a course, courses that cover multiple competencies, an internship, or other activities established for developing these competencies. Therefore, students should review program coursework as well as other program experiences to evaluate the training of I-O competencies.

Applied Experiences

In addition to coursework, applied experiences (see Chapter 4 of this book) might include internships, practica, consulting work, and applied research. Some programs have university-based consulting centers (see Chapter 6 of this book) where I-O graduate students work on consulting projects for organizational clients under faculty supervision. An understanding of the types of internships and other applied experiences offered by a program can suggest the types of jobs program graduates obtain after graduation. In addition, potential students can request information on the jobs of program graduates. Prospective students aspiring to applied research positions should ensure there are ample opportunities for research experience in the master's program.

Emphases

Some programs will clearly describe themselves as I- or O-focused, or as a balanced I-O program. If not, reviewing the program description, coursework, applied activities, and faculty publications and presentations will help identify the program's emphasis. I-O master's programs typically make it clear whether they are a terminal master's program or a predoctoral program.

Thesis or No Thesis

As previously mentioned, most I-O master's programs offer a thesis option, suggesting that most programs see value in students completing a thesis project (for more detail on the benefits of a thesis, see Chapter 5 of this book). A student who is already employed or has work experience completing applied projects may gain less from a thesis than other master's students who need to further develop their skills in project management, technical writing, data management and analyses, and so forth (Shultz & Kottke, 1996). The thesis content expertise as well as thesis-related skills may provide an advantage in the interview process and in the job market.

Graduate Assistantships and Tuition Waivers

Many, but not all, I-O master's programs offer graduate assistantships and tuition waivers. Both are more common in full-time programs than in part-time or online programs where many of the graduate students are already employed. A graduate assistantship offers a stipend for working with faculty either as a research assistant or a teaching assistant. Specific assistantship duties depend on the faculty member's research program and/or teaching load. Typically, assistantships are part time and range from 10 to 20 hours a week. Stipends vary greatly across programs. Assistantships typically are limited in number and are awarded on a competitive basis. Tuition waivers may be full or partial waivers and also vary greatly across programs. Some programs offer out-of-state tuition waivers or "e-rates" for online programs, such that students pay the significantly lower in-state tuition. Information on assistantships and tuition waivers can be found in the information provided by various I-O master's programs found on the SIOP GTP webpage. It is unlikely assistantships and tuition waivers will cover the full cost of attending a master's program; most graduate students also need some form of financial aid.

Program Faculty

Students should review the training and research program of core and supporting program faculty. Although it is possible to deliver a strong master's program with relatively few full-time core I-O faculty, the success of the program will depend on faculty background, how many students are admitted, and whether a thesis is required. Support faculty might teach some required courses such as a quantitative psychologist teaching research methods or psychometrics, or a social psychologist teaching group dynamics. A larger number of full-time I-O faculty typically provides greater opportunity for applied experiences and I-O research. In contrast, some programs rely on adjunct faculty who generally teach but are not involved with research or available to supervise applied experiences.

In addition, students can gauge faculty involvement with the field of I-O through their presence at SIOP or other conferences. All SIOP conference programs, accessible from the SIOP website, are searchable by author/presenter name. Regular conference presentation is an indicator that faculty members are active in the profession and should be familiar with current issues presented at conferences. Students can directly inquire about conference participation if this information is not apparent from accessible information.

Equally important for students pursuing practitioner jobs is evidence of faculty and student engagement in applied projects and consulting activities. Many I-O faculty engage in applied organizational projects and other consulting activities that provide I-O master's students with applied experience without the benefit of a consulting center. If the program has an affiliated consulting center, it will likely be featured on the program's website. Again, prospective graduate students should inquire if such opportunities are not apparent on the program website.

Part-Time or Full-Time Study?

I-O master's programs differ in total credit hours required (e.g., 32 to 45). A student would need to take eight or nine credit hours each fall and spring semester to finish a 34- to 36-credits degree in the typical two-year span. Some programs require summer courses such as internship. Other programs include a combination of day and evening classes, implement an accelerated term (e.g., four- or eight-week class rotations), or offer all-evening classes in hopes of reducing time to degree completion and attracting working professionals (Husson & Kennedy, 2003). Yet, graduate classes are often offered on a fixed schedule—specific days, times, and semesters.

The option to go "part time" (i.e., attending fewer classes each term) may become *the* determining factor of possible programs depending on students' circumstances. Demands on student time include homework, readings, research, library and/or lab time, possible internship or consulting opportunities, and working on milestones (e.g., thesis, comprehensive exam). Some courses might require a minimum of four study hours for every hour of class (12 hours for each three-credit course) or more *per week*. Students should inquire about the flexibility to vary enrollment each semester, as needed. Similarly, an online degree program may be the best or only option for a student who is geographically restricted. Such programs can vary widely in delivery, structure, requirements, opportunities, and "feel." Students should evaluate the program delivery method in terms of quality, availability, and student preferences.

Delivery Method

Traditional I-O master's programs are full-time programs of study offered on campus, and the professor and students meet together in the same place and at the same time. These brick-and-mortar programs are still predominant, but there has been growth in online programs in recent years.

Online programs can be completely synchronous, where the professor and students meet virtually at the same time for a session, as in a face-to-face class. Most online programs use some to total asynchrony. Totally asynchronous courses do not meet at set times. Professors in such programs often prerecord lectures (e.g., voiceover PowerPoint presentations in modular format, videos, or recorded virtual classes). Content could be primarily text-based with interaction limited to a discussion board. In some asynchronous courses there can be required or optional synchronous activities throughout the semester. Some traditional in-seat classes might be "hybrid" or "blended," in which there are recorded lectures and/or other online activities, especially when associated with an online program. Online programs can be independent of traditional programs, or the online and in-seat students interact in the same class (either synchronously, asynchronously, or both).

Not all online programs are of high quality, but neither are all face-to-face programs. Numerous online I-O programs meet modern students' needs and maintain the same rigorous standards and expectations as quality face-to-face programs. Quality online programs may be some students' preferred (or only) option. Due to the prevalence of and demand for fully or partially online I-O programs, they must be included in any comparison. At this writing, SIOP is surveying online programs in order to provide more structured information about I-O programs delivered online. Students should find programs that meet their needs and then evaluate quality, as previously discussed, applying the same standards regardless of delivery method. Next we compare traditional and online I-O master's program features and components.

Lectures and Seminars

In a face-to-face class, the professor and students meet together. As the professor provides information and asks questions, it is possible to gain immediate feedback from the students (usually orally or visually) about the material and the students gain the immediate reaction of the professor; questions can be addressed as they arise. Similarly, in a seminar, there is a synergy based on concomitant input from all participants.

In a virtual class, available students log into a video meeting "room" or live class and interact as in a face-to-face class, including oral or text conversation, slideshows, demonstrations through screen sharing, or doodling on a virtual whiteboard. For unavailable students, recording these virtual classes allows them to benefit from the live experience while maintaining asynchrony.

Online classes that use only discussion boards or recorded PowerPoint lectures do not have this same level of immediate feedback. Depending on time requirements for responding, there can be lively online discussions, but they might not reach the dynamic level likely in an in-seat class. In order to ensure a thorough discussion, assignments often include specific instructions on when and how often to respond. In addition, the professor and students must proactively seek feedback. Only when in-class students and synchronous online students are involved during the recording of online lectures is there immediate oral or written feedback for the instructor, but that is often a subset of the total class. Similarly, the instructor only receives visual feedback in sessions that include in-class and/or synchronous online students with a webcam.

Demonstrations

After presenting material on a topic, the instructor might ask students to apply the concepts (e.g., determining necessary reliability and validity in a scale or creating a situational interview question). In an in-seat class, the instructor might work with the students using handouts. Unless the students are graded on participation, it is possible to have a similar experience for online students. If there are both in-seat and online students participating, different computer web-based platforms (e.g., Google, Microsoft OneNote) allow for everyone to work on the same project; however, in-seat students will need computers and internet access. For completely asynchronous classes, posting activities into a discussion board allows students to work together; the instructor can later post a recorded demo of the activity for review.

Testing

For take-home or open-book exams, there is no real difference between in-class and online formats. When testing students with a timed exam, instructors in brick-and-mortar programs generally print the exam, bring it to class, and distribute, proctor, and collect the exam. For online programs, instructors upload the exam into the learning management software, set an availability window, and possibly use various agencies that provide minimal to live online exam proctoring (e.g., Examity, ProctorU). Other programs might use testing centers in the student's community. This expense is sometimes passed on to the students. If a student needs accommodations (e.g., to meet Americans with Disabilities Act regulations), increased time allotment or screen-reader formats are easily accommodated in either delivery method.

Student Presentations and Colloquia

Traditional programs often require students to present in class on a variety of topics. At other times, there might be colloquia in which students are expected to present. If the goal is to have an open, real-time discussion (i.e., colloquium, class), this is a challenge for online programs. Online students would need to be present at a particular day and time, and given that online students often work (often full time), this creates scheduling issues. Advance notice and planning may allow for coordination of online and in-seat students' schedules.

If the course is completely asynchronous, students can record and upload their video presentation to a discussion board. In turn, the students can be required to discuss and provide asynchronous feedback about the presentation itself or the topic. The main difference in this course activity between online and in-seat programs is the use of technology and more time allotted for asynchronous communication. If online and in-seat students are in the same class, this process could be required of all students. The use of technology and asynchronous communication might feel extremely different, lacking the type of community that is generally inherent in brick-and-mortar programs.

Applied Experiences

Applied experiences such as applied course projects, practica, and internships are invaluable training for I-O master's students and are a core component of many brick-and-mortar I-O master's programs. Faculty requiring applied course projects generally must guide student selection of their project or develop and provide the project (i.e., establish the organizational connections and settle the agreement with the organization concerning the requirements for the applied project). The same would be true for online faculty; however, the online faculty will need to be deliberate about scheduling meetings with the students, as the students and faculty generally do not meet regularly in class. This requires the coordination of faculty and student schedules, which could include evenings and weekends. Complications develop when the applied projects require students to meet with organizational stakeholders or visit the organization site for observation. Virtual meetings can occur with the organization, but scheduling is often limited to business hours. If there are in-seat students and online students in the same class working on group projects, it is possible to divide the responsibilities of the project, if appropriate. The coordination of groups with all online students or a mix of in-seat and online students is another consideration, as these students could be in multiple time zones and even different continents. Planning, coordinating, and establishing creative ways to offer applied projects might be impossible for faculty in fully online programs.

Generally, for practica and internships, there is faculty oversight or mentoring, which often includes regular meetings with the students. Recurring meetings can be scheduled with either brick-and-mortar or online faculty. Because the faculty member often identifies the applied opportunities, the opportunities may not be in the location where an online student resides. In these cases, it would be the student's responsibility to find an internship in his or her community.

Consulting

Consulting opportunities generally require students to be present to meet with clients, give presentations, collect data, or view the work site. This creates an obstacle for online students. In some cases, it is possible to use technology for client meetings, presentations, and data collection, but the online student would not be able to truly experience the work site virtually. If the consulting project involves a group, it is possible that tasks can be delegated, but it would be important to develop activities that allow online students the opportunity to gain observational experiences.

Research Opportunities and Theses

Conducting research in traditional programs generally requires multiple meetings and informal conversations between the faculty member and student (e.g., a discussion during lunch). The ability to spontaneously meet and discuss topics can be a great advantage, one that does not typically occur with online students. In addition, if the research requires the use of an on-campus laboratory, this might reduce or preclude online student involvement. Again, it will depend on whether there is a group of research students who can divide the project responsibilities; however, the online students still will not have the in-lab experience.

Technology available for data collection (e.g., monitors, iPads, Qualtrics) will enable online students to conduct research. The biggest challenge is ensuring there is sufficient contact between the student and faculty member. That is, it may be more difficult to "track down" an online student than an on-campus student. Therefore, faculty should establish ground rules and students must proactively maintain contact with the faculty member and research team.

For online student theses, even if the research can be conducted online, the ability to meet informally with each committee member, as well as for the proposal and defense meetings, might be a challenge; however, technology exists for simulated face-to-face meetings. We recommend that meetings with faculty about research include video.

Mentoring and Advising

In both brick-and-mortar and online programs, formal mentoring and advising occur in formal meetings. On-campus students have the advantage of spontaneous conversations with faculty about career options and other advice. Faculty and students in online programs should be more deliberate in scheduling meetings; however, it is possible to create some online spontaneity. For example, an online student or faculty member can initiate a spontaneous conversation using communication technologies such as Zoom, Cisco, or Skype for synchronous video, voice, or text-based interactions. Spontaneous synchronous video conversations are most similar to on-campus spontaneous conversations. Some programs might develop a culture for impromptu communication that occurs whenever messages are received or is limited to business hours.

Communication

Communication in traditional programs is typically face to face in the classroom, one-on-one meetings, or group meetings, and can be formal or informal, although at times phone or text-only messages may be used. Therefore, a heavy reliance on text communication (e.g., email) in an online program might restrict the quality of the communication, even though it seems easier. Online faculty can use communication technologies that allow for face-to-face meetings but, similar to text communications, these meetings generally occur one on one, which requires more faculty time dedicated to communicating with students. Using technologies such as Zoom, Cisco, or Skype, faculty can communicate with groups electronically. In addition, faculty can create electronic meeting spaces such as a Zoom channel for virtual meetings. These virtual meeting spaces provide all students (and faculty) a place for unscheduled discussions with online students as one would for on-campus students, which can greatly enhance informal conversation and interaction. For students, this practice also may enhance perceptions of faculty members' approachability and commitment to their online students. We strongly recommend students determine the forms of communication used in an online I-O master's program of interest.

Program Community and Social Events

In brick-and-mortar programs, students attend classes, work on projects, study, and socialize together (sometimes with the faculty). This community allows for informal discussions including topics related to I-O. Having such a support network can be extremely beneficial for graduate students. Developing program community and social events for online students is the biggest challenge. With encouragement, online students will communicate with each other, but that community is often not as well developed as for on-campus students. Distance students need to make a concerted effort to know students in their cohort beyond program or course requirements. Strategies to increase the sense of program community and social interaction include coordinating attendance and gatherings at I-O conferences or events, encouraging students to connect with each other via social media platforms (e.g., GroupMe, Facebook, LinkedIn), video-based virtual office hours with multiple students, group Zoom channels, and virtual lunch breaks and happy hours where attendees can log in to a scheduled video, voice, or text-based session to discuss professional and/or personal topics in an informal environment.

Preparing for Master's Programs

Admission into an I-O master's program is competitive and requires a strong academic background with appropriate experiences. The following suggestions provide guidance for developing a competitive application for I-O master's programs.

Courses

The strongest undergraduate background for an I-O master's is an undergraduate degree in psychology, perhaps with some business courses. A business degree is appropriate as long as the student has background in research methods and statistics and a sufficient number of psychology courses to grasp foundational material (Shoenfelt, Stone, & Kottke, 2015). Therefore, in addition to psychology courses, students should take courses in behavioral statistics, research methods and, if available, tests and measurements, organizational psychology (or organizational behavior in the business school), industrial psychology, or a combined I-O survey course. Other courses that prepare students for studying I-O include social, cognitive, and personality psychology and management and/or business courses (e.g., HR; Shoenfelt et al., 2015).

Experience

Research experience may strengthen a graduate application. To become involved in research, undergraduates should learn about faculty research programs, identify faculty with whom they would like to work, and inquire about research opportunities with the faculty member. Faculty typically are eager to work with interested and motivated students. Learning the process of conducting research is more important than the actual research topic. Often, conducting research leads to a conference presentation and/or authorship on a publication, which are good experiences and résumé builders. Attending a conference further increases student knowledge and demonstrates interest in the field.

Students should consider internships or field experience, typically in HR (see Chapter 4 of this book and SIOP's Career page). Student membership in SIOP, the Society for Human Resource Management, or other relevant organizations (e.g., psychology club; Psi Chi, psychology's International Honor Society) provides additional experience. It is more important to be actively involved (e.g., leadership role, helping with activities) in fewer organizations than to join multiple organizations and not participate. Prospective students can discuss their involvement in these organizations in interviews and in their personal statement.

Grade-Point Average

Generally, a minimum grade-point average (GPA) of 3.0 is required for graduate school admission, but some programs have lower or higher cut scores of 2.5 or 3.5 (Tett, Walser, Brown, Simonet, & Tonidandel, 2013c). In some programs, higher scores on the Graduate Record Examination (GRE) can compensate for a lower GPA and vice versa. Students meeting the minimum GPA may not be admitted if the applicant pool is strong (i.e., all applicants have 3.5 or higher GPAs). The mean acceptance rate for master's programs is just over 40% in psychology departments, but only 20% in business departments (Tett et al., 2013c). Students can inquire about GPA and GRE statistics for a program's recent cohorts.

Although GPA is important, a high GPA does not guarantee admission; students need relevant experience, as previously discussed, to stand out from other applicants. Undergraduates should begin developing the skills that will be needed as an I-O graduate student and practitioner, including oral and written communication, interpersonal interaction, and business or consulting skills, and must avoid counterproductive work behaviors such as plagiarism (Salter & O'Malley, 2014). Essentially, students need to take the right courses and gain the right experience, must do quality work, and must be professional and ethical.

GRE

The SIOP graduate program webpage gives average GRE Verbal and Quantitative scores for each graduate program. Many universities offer a GRE preparation class, or students can purchase study materials from reputable publishers (e.g., Kaplan, Princeton Review) and directly from the Educational Testing Service (ETS), which administers the GRE and provides free materials. Students should confirm that their preparation includes computerized practice tests that replicate the format of the actual GRE administration. We recommend against taking the GRE "cold" (i.e., not studying or preparing) just to see how one might do.

The GRE is a computer-adaptive test whereby exam items are generated based on how a test taker scored on the previous item. A correct answer on an item of medium difficulty will result in a more difficult subsequent item; the converse also is true. This difficulty adjustment continues throughout the test so that each test taker receives a unique set of exam items. A seemingly difficult exam could be an indication that the test taker is doing well and, consequently, is presented with increasingly difficult items.

At the end of the exam, before the test is scored, test takers must decide whether to report scores to their identified schools or to cancel them (ETS, n.d.). If cancelled, test takers do not see their scores. Unless the test taker is fairly certain of a poor score (e.g., quite ill while taking the test, frequently guessing answers), scores generally should be reported. Those who did not score well would then have a baseline to further hone preparation. GRE scores expire after five years (ETS, n.d.). Most schools requiring the GRE consider the last attempt, the highest attempt, or an average of all attempts. (This is another reason not to take the test without preparing.) It is acceptable to ask a point of contact how multiple attempts on the GRE are handled by an admissions committee.

Applying to Master's Programs

Students should have a tiered list of potential programs based on admission requirements and acceptance rates; that is, master's programs for which it is fairly easy to gain acceptance, those that are more competitive (but attainable), and those that are more exclusive. Students should apply only to programs they would consider attending if they are accepted.

Tracking Applications and Deadlines

We highly recommend that students create a tracking system for their master's program applications. An Excel spreadsheet is easily organized and can be updated as progress occurs. The following are variables to track.

Basic Program Information
The student should list the name of the program, home department, school name, application deadline, and whether materials should be mailed, emailed, or uploaded electronically. References will need to submit their letter of recommendation early if it is to be mailed versus uploaded to an electronic system. Although most applications for fall admission are due early in the spring, actual deadlines vary widely. Some programs may also offer spring and/or summer admissions (likely with fall deadlines). If this information is tracked using Excel, students can sort their applications by deadline or outstanding items.

Required Admissions Materials
Most I-O master's programs require scores on the GRE general exam, all undergraduate- and graduate-level transcripts, letters of recommendation (usually three), a personal statement, and an application fee. Some programs also request a résumé, writing sample, or research statement. Different

notations in the tracking system can indicate submitted, requested, and incomplete items for each application to ensure all deadlines are met. Students should request materials (e.g., transcripts) at least a month before the deadline and should identify one or two dates within this timeframe to check to ensure requested items were sent and received. The admissions committee may remove incomplete or late applications from consideration.

Letters of Recommendation

Faculty members likely are the best source of recommendations as they generally know the type of information needed in a reference letter. Students should ask faculty who can write a strong letter that directly addresses student academic achievement, aptitude for graduate work, collegiality, work ethic, desire to be mentored, professionalism, research, writing, and other related characteristics. Working professionals applying to master's programs will likely need to ask supervisors to write letters but should have at least one academic reference, if possible. Recommendation letters can focus on the aforementioned attributes as well as skills in project management, leadership, time management, and delegation, for example. It is critical that students ask references if they are willing to write a letter well ahead of the due date (e.g., one month). Students should provide letter writers with basic program information, deadlines, method of delivery, a personal statement, strengths of the student relative to the program, particular attributes or projects the writer could highlight for particular programs, and their relationship to the letter writer (e.g., course taken, research experience). When a student demonstrates this level of professionalism and preparedness in requesting a letter, writers may be more inclined to write a good letter. If a potential letter writer suggests any reason the student should ask someone else, students should heed this advice as it likely portends a weak letter from this reference. Religious leaders, peers, family, or friends are not appropriate references.

Personal Statement

In a personal statement, students should address any program-suggested topics as well as why they are applying to that particular program, demonstrating that they researched the program; why they are interested in the field of I-O; and experiences relevant to their prospective I-O master's training. Students should ensure that their personal statement, and all interactions with program contacts, are professional. Finally, statements should fall within the suggested page limit; if none is given, we suggest a two-page maximum.

Admissions Decisions

Admissions committees review applications and make offers of admission to their top applicants, as programs cannot admit unlimited numbers of students. Therefore, decision letters indicate denial of admission, pending or waitlist status, or an admission offer. Highly successful applicants will receive multiple acceptances and will need to consider and compare each offer (e.g., funding) before making their final decision to attend. Once a student accepts an offer, they should notify the other programs who have extended admission offers, enabling those programs to offer a position to another applicant on their waitlist.

Conclusions

Identifying, applying to, and being admitted to a high-quality, well-matched I-O master's program requires extensive effort and an intentional strategy for success. When choosing a program, students should consider the program's quality and characteristics, overall fit between themselves and the program, and specific characteristics of the offer. The recommendations in this chapter should assist prospective I-O master's students and their advisors in identifying appropriate I-O programs, reviewing program options, preparing well, and submitting professional applications that result in admission to an I-O master's program that will meet the student's career goals.

References

Acikgoz, Y., Huelsman, T. J., Swets, J. L., Dixon, A. R., Jeffer, S. N., Olsen, D. R., & Ross, A. (2018). The cream of the crop: Student and alumni perceptions of I-O psychology master's degree program quality. *The Industrial-Organizational Psychologist*, 55(4). http://my.siop.org/tip/jan18/editor/ArtMID/13745/ArticleID/334/The-Cream-of-the-Crop-Student-and-Alumni-Perceptions-of-I-O-Psychology-Masters-Degree-Program-Quality

Educational Testing Service [ETS]. (n.d.). Frequently asked questions about the GRE general test. https://www.ets.org/gre/revised_general/faq/

Erffmeyer, E. S., & Mendel, R. M. (1990). Master's level training in industrial/organizational psychology: A case study of the perceived relevance of graduate training.

Professional Psychology: Research and Practice, 21, 405–408. https://doi.org/10.1037/0735-7028.21.5.405

Gasser, M., Butler, A., Waddilove, L., & Tan, R. (2004). Defining the profession of industrial-organizational psychology. *The Industrial-Organizational Psychologist, 42*(2), 15–20. https://doi.org/10.1037/e578782011-002

Husson, W. J., & Kennedy, T. (2003). Developing and maintaining accelerated degree programs within traditional institutions. *New Directions for Adult & Continuing Education, 97*, 51–61. https://doi.org/10.1002/ace.88

Kottke, J. L., Shoenfelt, E. L., & Stone, N. J. (2014). Educating industrial-organizational psychologists: Lessons learned from master's programs. *Industrial and Organizational Psychology: Perspectives on Science and Practice, 7*, 26–31. https://doi.org/10.1111/iops.12099

Lowe, R. H. (1993). Master's programs in industrial/organizational psychology: Current status and a call for action. *Professional Psychology: Research and Practice, 24*, 27–34. https://doi.org/10.1037/0735-7028.24.1.27

Salter, N. P., & O'Malley, A. L. (2014). A good graduate industrial-organizational education begins in undergraduate classrooms. *Industrial and Organizational Psychology: Perspectives on Science and Practice, 7*, 15–84. https://doi.org/10.1111/iops.12096

Shoenfelt, E. L. (2019). I-O master's graduate survey. Survey conducted for E. L. Shoenfelt (Ed.) (in press), *Mastering the job market: Career issues for master's-level industrial-organizational psychologist*. New York: Oxford University Press.

Shoenfelt, E. L., Stone, N. J., & Kottke, J. L. (2013). Internships: An established mechanism for increasing employability. *Industrial and Organizational Psychology: Perspectives on Science and Practice, 6*, 24–28. https://doi.org/10.1111/iops.12004

Shoenfelt, E. L., Stone, N. J., & Kottke, J. L. (2015). Industrial-organizational and human factors graduate program admission: Information for undergraduate advisors. *Teaching of Psychology, 42*, 79–82. https://doi.org/10.1177/0098628314562683

Shultz, K. S., & Kottke, J. L. (1996). The master's thesis in applied psychology training. *Teaching of Psychology, 23*, 166–168. https://doi.org/10.1177/009862839602300307

Society for Human Resource Management. (2018). *SHRM human resource curriculum: Guidebook and templates for undergraduate and graduate programs*. https://www.shrm.org/certification/for-organizations/academic-alignment/Documents/2019%20Curriculum%20Guidebook%20Update_FNL.pdf

Society for Industrial and Organizational Psychology, Inc. (2016). *Guidelines for education and training in industrial-organizational psychology*. Bowling Green, OH: Author.

Tett, R. P., Brown, C., & Walser, B. (2014). The 2011 SIOP graduate program benchmarking survey part 7: Theses, dissertations, and performance expectations. *The Industrial-Organizational Psychologist, 51*(4), 62–73. https://doi.org/10.1037/e570072013-005

Tett, R. P., Brown, C., Walser, B., & Tonidandel, S. (2013b). The 2011 SIOP graduate program benchmarking survey part 4: Internships. *The Industrial-Organizational Psychologist, 51*(1), 40–52. https://doi.org/10.1037/e570072013-005

Tett, R. P., Brown, C., Walser, B., Tonidandel, S., & Simonet, D. V. (2013a). The 2011 SIOP graduate program benchmarking survey part 5: Comprehensive exams. *The Industrial-Organizational Psychologist, 51*(2), 57–70. https://doi.org/10.1037/e570072013-005

Tett, R. P., Walser, B., Brown, C., Simonet, D. V., & Tonidandel, S. (2013c). 2011 SIOP graduate program benchmarking survey part II: Admissions standards and procedures.

The Industrial-Organizational Psychologist, 50(3), 13–32. https://doi.org/10.1037/e520182013-002

U.S. Department of Education. (2019). Accreditation in the United States. https://www2.ed.gov/admins/finaid/accred/accreditation.html#Overview

Vodanovich, S. J., Morganson, V. J., & Kass, S. J. (2018). Ranking I-O master's programs using objective data from I-O coordinators. *The Industrial-Organizational Psychologist, 55*(4). http://my.siop.org/tip/jan18/editor/ArtMID/13745/ArticleID/333/Ranking-I-O-Masters-Programs-Using-Objective-Data-From-I-O-Coordinators1

3

The Industrial-Organizational Master's Degree Curriculum

Considerations for Teaching Competencies in the SIOP *Guidelines for Education and Training in Industrial-Organizational Psychology*

Timothy J. Huelsman and Linda Rhoades Shanock

The previous two chapters introduced industrial-organizational (I-O) psychology master's programs and provided information about applying to graduate school in I-O psychology. This chapter introduces guidelines for the I-O psychology master's degree curriculum set forth by the Society for Industrial and Organizational Psychology (SIOP). In 2016, SIOP published the latest edition of its *Guidelines for Education and Training in Industrial-Organizational Psychology* (hereafter *Guidelines*). The *Guidelines* take a competency-based approach to describing the content of graduate training in I-O psychology. Their express purpose is to "aid faculty and curriculum planners in the design of master's- and doctoral-level graduate programs in I-O Psychology" (SIOP, 2016, p. 1). The purpose of this chapter is to (a) provide an overview of the *Guidelines*, (b) describe some delivery options for developing the competencies in the *Guidelines*, and (c) describe how the characteristics of a master's program may present opportunities or challenges in addressing the *Guidelines*.

An Overview of the *Guidelines*

SIOP originally published guidelines for doctoral education in 1973–1974 and issued a revised set in 1985 (Gibson, Allen, Payne, Huelsman, & Fritsch, 2018a; Gibson, Payne, Morgan, & Allen, 2018b). A 1999 revision produced separate documents for master's- and doctoral-level training. Several

Timothy J. Huelsman and Linda Rhoades Shanock, *The Industrial-Organizational Master's Degree Curriculum*
In: *Mastering Industrial-Organizational Psychology*. Edited by: Elizabeth L. Shoenfelt, Oxford University Press (2020).
© Society for Industrial and Organizational Psychology. DOI: 10.1093/oso/9780190071141.003.0003.

years ago, the SIOP Education and Training Committee (comprising academics and practitioners at both the master's and doctoral levels) created a Guidelines Subcommittee to serve as caretaker of the *Guidelines*, including making revisions in accordance with directives from the American Psychological Association (2004). Over the past several years, this subcommittee worked to revise the *Guidelines* into their present form. The revision process has included numerous discussions at SIOP's annual meetings (including program director meetings and executive board special sessions), updates in SIOP's quarterly publication *The Industrial-Organization Psychologist* (*TIP*), and empirical efforts aimed at identifying the domains necessary to ensure successful careers in I-O psychology (see, for example, Payne, Morgan, & Allen, 2015). Information from these sources and the discussion stimulated by them were considered when arriving at the final set of competencies.

The largest part of the *Guidelines* is the recommended areas of competence, which describes the 26 competencies to be developed by I-O psychology graduate programs. It is beyond the scope of this chapter to present these competencies in detail, but enumerating them and their organization is essential (Table 3.1 gives the full list).

The competencies are separated into three broad domains. The first domain, General Knowledge and Skills, comprises six foundational competencies essential to the field, including ethical, legal, and diversity issues, fields of psychology, professional skills, research methods, and statistics. The second domain, Core Content, comprises 18 competencies that may be considered the signature areas of I-O psychology. The third domain, Related Areas of Competence, comprises two competencies that are on the periphery of I-O psychology (consumer behavior, human factors).

A striking feature of the current *Guidelines* is that this single document addresses both master's *and* doctoral training rather than having separate guidelines for each level of training as in the previous version. Even so, the current *Guidelines* recognize differences between (terminal) master's and doctoral training, specifying that master's programs may be distinguished from doctoral programs in three ways: master's programs are more limited in their breadth and depth of training, they have a greater focus on specific content and application than on research skills, and they prepare their students more for applied jobs than for academic roles. None of these distinctions indicates meaningful content differences based on level of education; therefore, there is a single set of competencies (SIOP, 2016).

Table 3.1 Recommended Areas of Competence for Graduate Training in I-O Psychology (per the SIOP *Guidelines*)

General Knowledge and Skills

1. Ethical, Legal, Diversity, and International Issues
2. Fields of Psychology
3. History and Systems of Psychology
4. Professional Skills (Communication, Business/Research Development, Consulting, and Project-Management Skills)
5. Research Methods
6. Statistical Methods/Data Analysis

Core Content

7. Attitude Theory, Measurement, and Change
8. Career Development
9. Criterion Theory and Development
10. Groups and Teams
11. Human Performance
12. Individual Assessment
13. Individual Differences
14. Job Evaluation and Compensation
15. Job/Task/Work Analysis, Competency Modeling, and Classification
16. Judgment and Decision-Making
17. Leadership and Management
18. Occupational Health and Safety
19. Organization Development
20. Organization Theory
21. Performance Appraisal/Management
22. Personnel Recruitment, Selection, and Placement
23. Training: Theory, Delivery, Program Design, and Evaluation
24. Work Motivation

Related Areas of Competence

25. Consumer Behavior
26. Human Factors

In taking a competency-based approach, the *Guidelines* are rooted in the scientist-practitioner model that emphasizes focusing on science and application of science in all the content areas for master's and doctoral education, regardless of career path (SIOP, 2016). The *Guidelines* state that applying the information learned in each content area gives students familiarity with the limits and challenges of the topics and techniques; this is different from, and just as important as, learning the content theoretically. The emphasis on a scientist-practitioner model has important implications for program design and implementation. Next, we turn to a discussion of curriculum options to provide ideas for developing these competencies within master's programs.

Options for Developing I-O Competencies in Master's Programs

The *Guidelines* describe essential competencies I-O graduate students should develop but do not prescribe any specific curriculum. The *Guidelines* do suggest strategies programs might use to develop student competencies: formal coursework, independent readings/study, supervised experience (and field research), on-the-job-training, modeling/observation, involvement in funded research, and collaborative research. Further, the *Guidelines* provide a table with suggestions on what strategies are best suited for mastery of each of the competencies. Unsurprisingly, all competencies may be addressed by multiple strategies, and almost all strategies are appropriate for almost all competencies.

It is likely most of the strategies described in the *Guidelines* are familiar to I-O faculty (and students). However, the nature of master's programs provides some unique challenges in employing these modes of training. The *Guidelines* recognize there is considerable heterogeneity among graduate programs in I-O psychology; but, even at the risk of overgeneralizing, it may be useful to highlight some of the differences between master's and doctoral programs in psychology. Note that in these comparisons we focus only on differences in psychology-based programs, not those in business schools.

Tett et al. (2012), in the first of an eight-part graduate program benchmarking effort, reported there are differences between master's and doctoral programs in the number of students (number of yearly graduates; master's $M = 10.5$, doctoral $M = 3.5$), number of full-time core faculty (master's $M = 3.5$, doctoral $M = 4.7$), and number of courses taught per year by adjuncts (master's $M = 2.5$, doctoral $M = 1.7$). It likely is a safe assumption that teaching expectations for master's faculty will be greater (e.g., a 3-3 load) than for doctoral faculty (e.g., a 2-2 load). To offset the greater teaching expectations, master's faculty likely have research expectations that are not as great as those for doctoral faculty. Faculty associated with both master's and doctoral programs may have expectations that do not fit either of these patterns.

Students in master's and doctoral programs have different characteristics. Tett et al. (2012) reported that a higher proportion of master's students (90.9%) seek applied (versus academic) jobs than do doctoral students (67.2%). Consistent with this, Tett, Brown, Walser, and Tonidandel (2013) reported that master's programs are more likely to require internships (58.8%) than are doctoral programs (33.3%), and Tett, Walser, and Brown (2014) suggested that the preparation provided in master's programs favors careers in practice rather than in academic settings. Providing additional data supporting this point, Tett et al. (2014) reported that theses are required in 40% of master's programs, are optional in 47.7%, and are not even offered in 12.7%. This is in stark contrast to doctoral programs where, unsurprisingly, 100% of programs required formal research activities (theses/dissertations). Finally, faculty in master's programs have fewer research expectations of their students (e.g., peer-reviewed publications, brown-bag attendance, independent research) than do their counterparts in doctoral programs (Tett, Brown, & Walser, 2014).

Financial and other resources may be more limited in the typical master's program compared to the typical doctoral program. Tett, Walser, Brown, Tonidandel, and Simonet (2014) reported that doctoral programs (89.7%) are more likely to provide assistantships to their students than are master's programs (71.4%). Doctoral assistantships ($13,908) are more lucrative than master's assistantships ($6,684). Considering additional awards like tuition waivers and reimbursements for travel, research, and other expenses, the average total award for doctoral students ($23,216) is almost twice that for master's students ($12,409). Fellowships and scholarships differ, with doctoral students (52%) more likely to receive them than are master's students (12%), and with larger average awards in doctoral ($15,859) than in master's programs ($5,932). Tett et al. assessed the availability of 18 other resources and found that doctoral students had greater availability of university-sponsored health insurance, printing, photocopying, literature search platforms, and access to computers.

The resources available to doctoral students may allow them to fully engage in their program and avoid outside work. In contrast, the more limited resources of master's students may increase the likelihood that they must hold outside jobs to support their education or go to graduate school part time (whereas most doctoral students are full time). Either of these outcomes could limit the ability of master's students to fully engage in the development opportunities offered by their programs. Further, based on the first 10 master's and doctoral programs listed on the SIOP website, master's programs require fewer credit hours (38 on average) than doctoral programs (78 on average). Master's students are in their graduate programs approximately only two years, allowing even less time for career preparation.

Given these differences between master's and doctoral programs (and recognizing the heterogeneity among programs), faculty in master's programs may grapple with how best to develop the competencies described in the *Guidelines*. We next discuss strategies that can be employed by master's programs, including some prescriptive advice based on our experiences with master's programs in I-O psychology.

Formal Coursework

Formal coursework is probably the dominant method used to develop student competencies in most master's programs. Given the limited time students spend in I-O master's programs, the main challenge with coursework is the tradeoff between breadth and depth. For instance, Groups and Teams is one of the competencies in the *Guidelines*. A master's program may cover theory and research relevant to this competency in a course titled *Organizational Psychology* that also covers material relevant to other competencies such as Attitudes, Judgment and Decision-Making, Leadership, and Work Motivation, to name just a few. Many master's programs may supplement the coverage offered through coursework with other opportunities to gain depth in particular competencies through outside-the-classroom experiences. In their efforts to assess course coverage of the competencies in their programs, we encourage faculty to engage in mapping their courses onto the competencies (Gibson et al. [2018a] developed an Excel-based matrix to facilitate this process; this matrix is described in the concluding paragraphs of this chapter). This competency mapping may ensure that, for example, the "O" competencies all are covered in the "O" class(es) rather than simply focusing on the topics a particular instructor favors.

Approximately 41% of master's programs require a comprehensive exam (Tett, Brown, Walser, Tonidandel, & Simonet, 2013), and, in many cases, preparation materials are provided that may include guidance on material that students may not have covered in their coursework. In such cases, study materials can be assigned to help students round out learning competencies when studying for the exam. Faculty can help by holding review or other discussion sessions, especially for content not covered in courses.

Independent Readings and Independent Study

Independent readings and independent study are described in the *Guidelines* as methods in which the student assumes responsibility for, and commitment to achieving, learning objectives for a particular content area (or areas) under the supervision of a qualified mentor (SIOP, 2016). Given the student-to-faculty ratios present in many master's programs, these independent study activities are not time effective and thus are not likely to be widely used. In unique circumstances independent study could work for a student who wanted to gain competence in an area where a particular faculty member is currently engaged in research, teaching, or consulting. Or, if a student misses a course or a semester due to personal circumstances such as medical issues or family leave, the program could offer independent study as an option for making up the missed work. As an alternative to independent study, courses in sociology, management, public policy, education, or other fields may help round out competency development if relevant coursework is not offered in the I-O program.

Supervised Experience and Field Research

Supervised experience and field research are frequently employed in master's programs, especially the former. These activities are hands-on learning experiences such as internships and practica in which students gain skills and experience in settings that are similar to future work roles but that are not motivated primarily by compensation (SIOP, 2016). Internships are required in 58.8% of master's programs and are available in all but 3.8% of programs (Tett, Brown, Walser, & Tonidandel, 2013). Many programs also have affiliated organizations (institutes, centers, etc.) through which students get research, evaluation, and consulting experience. Although internships and some applied experiences may be compensated, given the typical level of compensation ($20 to $25 per hour, in our experience), it would be hard to argue that compensation is the *primary* motivation for engaging in these activities.

Internships and practica may be particularly well suited for specific competencies such as ethics, diversity, and professional skills (Shoenfelt, Kottke, & Stone, 2012). What may be less obvious is that certain Core Content competencies are likely to be targeted by master's-level internships (Shoenfelt, Stone, & Kottke, 2013). In our experience, students are much more likely to get internships that focus on industrial psychology and human resources tasks than the organizational psychology competencies. It may also be true that industrial psychology and human resources jobs are more readily available to master's-level graduates, which is something faculty (and students) should keep in mind.

Theses also fit into this category and are available in all but a small number of programs (Tett, Brown, & Walser, 2014). Theses and other research experiences offer the opportunity to develop one or more competencies in considerable depth. For master's programs, research activity may be less well suited to their students' applied interests and professional trajectory. However, theses and other research activities facilitate student growth beyond research method and statistics. Research activities also allow students to take a deep dive into one or more of the Core Content competencies that make up the corpus of I-O psychology. For example, if a student's thesis is on leadership, the student will need to master the content and background of literature on leadership as part of the thesis process. Master's graduates can use this expertise as a competitive advantage in the job market and can parlay it into serving as subject matter experts in the area they learned for their master's thesis work once in their applied jobs.

Faculty in master's programs should carefully consider the supervision of these in-depth experiences (Shoenfelt et al., 2012). The *Guidelines* state that meaningful professional supervision of these in-depth experiences must occur. Because master's I-O programs typically have a small number of faculty qualified to supervise these applied activities, it is essential that there is adequate institutional recognition and support for these important but time-consuming endeavors. For theses, this issue may present a faculty workload issue; however, students frequently are able to incorporate their thesis project into the ongoing research of program faculty. For internships, faculty may find it useful to develop and maintain relationships with partners in organizations outside the university. In our experience, program alumni, contacts at previous internship sites, or individuals in a faculty member's own professional network all may be tapped to provide qualified supervision of student field experiences.

An additional factor to attend to is the timelines specified by the *Guidelines*. The recommendation that research activities commence in the first year may be impractical in some master's programs. Similarly, the notion of an extensive supervised internship may be difficult to complete in the typically two-year calendar of a master's program.

On-the-Job Training

On-the-job-training is hands-on experience under the guidance of a qualified expert, similar to the supervised experiences of internships and practica we have already described. However, on-the-job-training is performed in conjunction with one's job and definitely involves compensation (SIOP, 2016). On-the-job-training in I-O psychology is an excellent way to further develop competencies learned in the classroom. On-the-job-training can provide a hands-on way to further develop general knowledge and skills (e.g., research methods and statistics, ethics and professional development) and experience in specific I-O Core Content domains (e.g., selection, talent management, organizational change, attitude surveys). However, this is not the norm for students in most master's programs. That is, master's students may either work at the university in an assistantship role not directly related to I-O psychology or work at part-time or full-time jobs outside the university setting that are not directly related to I-O psychology. Online I-O master's programs and evening programs targeting working adults would allow scheduling flexibility for students to try to find a full-time job in an I-O or HR position while in school. In these settings, thoughtful engagement while on a job related to I-O psychology or HR may represent a key way to gain competence. Similarly, for programs that do not incorporate internships or practica in their curriculum, faculty may advise students to seek out I-O–related opportunities during the summer or part time while in the program.

Modeling and Observation

Modeling and observation are unique among the *Guidelines'* options for gaining competence. The focus of modeling and observation is on students learning I-O skills by observing professionally qualified personnel as they go about their usual activities engaging in their job or projects (SIOP, 2016). The nature of this approach suggests that learning and professional development are important values in a program's culture. Faculty and others involved in the students' growth should recognize that their activities and behaviors do not go unnoticed by their students, who are looking to them as exemplars of professional behavior. In addition, this approach calls to mind one of the explicit values of the *Guidelines*: Students themselves are responsible for their own education and development (in addition to faculty). The strongest programs not only emphasize student responsibility, but also provide numerous opportunities for students to engage in the profession. This means programs facilitate field trips to businesses; encourage participation in SIOP, state/local I-O meetings, and meetings of other relevant professional organizations; publicize workshops and other development opportunities; invite guest speakers; involve alumni in the program; sponsor local networking events; pair students with I-O mentors; and other activities. Cognizant of the roles modeling and observation play in the development of competencies, programs can build these opportunities into the culture of their programs.

Involvement in Funded Research and Collaborative Research

The last two options for building competence, involvement in funded research and collaborative research, probably are more relevant to doctoral education than master's programs. That most master's programs do produce I-O researchers indicates there probably are adequate research opportunities in the Supervised Experience and Field Research category described earlier in the chapter to develop research competencies. I-O master's programs specifically designed to place students in doctoral programs and those focused on research may pay particular attention to these latter two strategies.

Opportunities and Challenges in Addressing the *Guidelines* in Master's Programs

The nature of master's programs may demand the emphasis of some training strategies and the deemphasis of others; however, master's programs are not homogeneous. The *Guidelines* briefly note potential differences among I-O master's programs (e.g., those providing predoctoral training versus those providing practitioner-oriented training); these differences have important implications for how these programs attempt to build competence in their students. In this section we describe some of the key differences among I-O master's programs that may influence how faculty address the *Guidelines*.

Traditional, Nontraditional, and Working Professional Students

Some programs tend to attract so-called traditional students; that is, students in their early 20s who come to graduate programs straight from or shortly after completing their undergraduate education (e.g., Francois, 2014). Some programs attract nontraditional or working professional students—that is, students who go back to school after three or more years of separation from college education (e.g., Francois, 2014). Some programs attract a mix of traditional and nontraditional, working professional students. Many students entering master's programs, whether traditional or nontraditional, plan to continue working while attending school, if possible (i.e., working professionals). Regardless, students may be attracted to a program based on characteristics such as the number of credit hours required, the availability of jobs nearby, whether it is a part-time or full-time program, and whether classes are offered in the evening or daytime. Despite the reasons students choose to attend a program, different types of students present challenges and opportunities with regard to developing I-O competencies.

Having primarily traditional students may be beneficial for faculty in I-O master's programs in terms of facilitating competency development. Traditional students usually have fresh knowledge of research methods and statistics (if retained!), fresh knowledge of core content from a basic course in I-O psychology or organizational behavior, and fresh knowledge in history and systems of psychology and other areas of psychology (if the student was a psychology major). Having recent knowledge of some of the competency areas in I-O psychology allows for a solid platform on which to build additional competencies. This foundation allows for greater depth to be developed in areas to which there is previous exposure, and greater breadth to be developed by exposing students to areas they did not encounter during undergraduate years. Traditional students also may be more of a blank slate regarding their professional development skills, allowing faculty to guide them in developing competency in I-O applications, ethics, research, and so forth without interference from conflicting practices acquired during years in the workforce.

However, challenges of working with traditional students may include their need for further maturation, the lack of full-time work experience during which some competencies already may have been developed (e.g., ethics, professional skills, appreciation of diversity), and a limited understanding of the context of work. These skills may need less emphasis in master's programs composed of nontraditional, working adults. Such nontraditional students may have a greater appreciation and desire for engaging fully in their graduate education given that they chose to come back to an I-O program after years of experience in the working world or having previous graduate education.

Having a mix of traditional and nontraditional students in a program can create unique challenges as the students will have varying needs for the development of particular skills. Nontraditional students may need more work in refreshing or developing their research methods or statistics skills (unless their work or previous graduate education developed such skills—in which case they may be ahead of traditional students). By contrast, traditional students might need more training in ethics and professional skill that nontraditional students already acquired from their job. Such challenges can be overcome by encouraging traditional students to engage in more of the professional development opportunities mentioned earlier, whereas nontraditional students may need to do some additional reading or workshops to develop core content in psychology or research methods and statistics. Though these examples are not meant to be overgeneralizations, we recommend I-O faculty think carefully about the type of students in their program and ways to meet their needs for competency development.

Standalone Master's and Master's Alongside PhD Programs

Many I-O master's programs are at universities that also have PhD programs in I-O psychology. Often, doctoral students earn a master's degree in I-O psychology along the way to their PhD in a rather seamless fashion, perhaps with some additional research or coursework required. In such programs, master's training looks essentially the same as doctoral training and is not as relevant to this volume on training master's students in I-O psychology. However, sometimes I-O master's programs that are run alongside PhD programs create challenges to competency development. One such challenge is that doctoral students tend to have more of a research focus while master's students tend to have more of an applied focus. This difference creates a challenging dynamic in formal coursework as the doctoral students often enjoy and desire discussions about theory and how to conduct research whereas terminal master's students often prefer discussions of how to apply the science and concepts. An additional challenge of offering side-by-side programs is that often the same I-O faculty are contributing to both programs. To the extent the programs do not overlap, they may require significant extra work on the part of the faculty to mentor and teach classes in both programs (particularly if classes are separated for the reasons mentioned earlier or if master's classes are held in the evenings and doctoral classes are held in the daytime, for example). These challenges add difficulty to helping master's students reach competency in the areas specified by the *Guidelines,* particularly if the competencies are not covered in formal coursework because faculty stretched thin by contributing to both master's and doctoral programs likely have little time to supervise independent studies or other experiences that could help with competency development.

Standalone master's programs provide the opportunity for the graduate focus to be only on master's-level interests and needs. The curriculum and associated experiences can be developed specifically for the needs of master's students. However, these programs have unique challenges too in that, without an affiliated doctoral program, often there is not the same breadth or frequency of coursework and there may be fewer faculty. There may be a need to use part-time faculty who may not be as familiar with the program's culture or the university's systems and, as such, may need more coaching. Master's programs often have fewer research-active faculty and resources for conducting research, and fewer overall resources outside of the classroom that may allow for richer master's-level training when it is offered alongside doctoral training.

Urban and Rural Environments

Perhaps one of the biggest factors in supervised experience (e.g., internships, on-the-job training, and modeling and observation) as curriculum delivery options for developing I-O competencies is whether the program is in an urban or rural setting. In our experience, urban settings afford much more in the way of I-O–related jobs and internships, as well as easier access to networking and professional development opportunities. In less urban settings, there typically just are not enough I-O professionals to allow for local groups to form, or enough organizations nearby to hire I-O psychology interns. If a program relies on adjunct faculty, they are likely to be in short supply in rural areas. To gain access to internship sites, students in rural areas may have to travel and live in a more urban area for the summer between their first and second year. To some extent, the ability of interns to work remotely may alleviate some of these challenges. But working from home may limit important elements of an intern's competency development, and often one is required to work at the physical location first before working remotely is allowed. On the other hand, a benefit of offering an I-O master's program in a rural area is that the students can stay focused on their graduate work.

I-O Psychology Versus Interdisciplinary Programs

Although the *Guidelines* should be commended as a way to make I-O psychology graduate training consistent enough to ensure that all students develop essential competencies for practice in I-O psychology, interdisciplinary graduate training also has been applauded as helpful for tackling the research and applied problems of the future (e.g., Boden, Borrego, & Newswander, 2011; Bridle, Vrieling, Cardillo, Araya, & Hinojosa, 2013). Such training may produce graduates with broad training in multiple research methods and analytic tools and exposure to additional theoretical paradigms beyond traditional I-O theories and schools of thought. Essentially, interdisciplinary training (which crosses disciplinary boundaries by synthesizing knowledge and methods from various disciplines) is argued to result in a larger and more varied toolkit for helping to solve real-world problems (e.g., Boden et al., 2011; Bridle et al., 2013). Thus, rather than representing a concern, heterogeneity among I-O master's programs in topics and methods and disciplines is beneficial to the field and to future practice of I-O psychology.

However, from the standpoint of trying to develop the 26 competencies listed in the *Guidelines*, interdisciplinary master's programs would face additional challenges beyond those experienced by solely I-O master's programs. Also, how do programs ensure the interdisciplinary coursework leads to the development of the competencies specified in the *Guidelines* given that such programs by their very nature need to be broad enough to develop competencies beyond I-O psychology as well as within it? Fields other than I-O psychology (e.g., organizational communication, organizational sociology, organizational behavior) have much to say about I-O topics (e.g., leadership, groups, and teams); thus, one could argue that an I-O–only view is not as rich for developing competencies as is an interdisciplinary view.

Second, interdisciplinary programs may require more coursework. For example, the first author's program complies with both the SIOP *Guidelines* and those of the Society for Human Resource Management, requiring 51 semester hours to address the recommended competencies—far more than the typical I-O master's program. Even so, students complete the program in a similar timeframe as a more typical program (21 months). This level of commitment is not for all students, particularly if they are employed.

Additional areas of competence may provide students with a competitive advantage in the job market, particularly because people in the business community may be more familiar with the additional areas of competence if they are from business schools (e.g., areas such as HR) than they are with I-O psychology. Thus, on the whole, we argue that being exposed to a wide range of perspectives is more helpful than hurtful in developing I-O competencies.

Classroom-Only, Online, and Hybrid Programs

Online and hybrid (partially online, partially in-person) I-O psychology programs are becoming increasingly prevalent; the SIOP website lists 22 online programs, 6 hybrid programs, and 91 classroom-only programs. As with other program characteristics, it is useful to discuss some potential challenges and opportunities of online versus classroom-only programs. Online programs provide students the opportunity for more flexibility in their schedules and allow them to live anywhere while attending the program. Students in such programs would likely have greater opportunity to develop the I-O competencies through work experiences and internships relative to classroom-only students. However, supervision of these experiences may challenge faculty associated with online programs, particularly if the work and internship sites are geographically dispersed and if the student–faculty ratio is high. For classroom-only programs, students may be constrained to geographical areas where relevant professional experiences are more difficult to identify. Students also may be constrained by a daytime class schedule. However, classroom-only programs may offer students a greater chance to engage in supervised research and professional activities given that students would be able to interact face to face with faculty and others. Similarly, in classroom-only programs a higher proportion of faculty may be full-time rather than adjunct instructors (who likely have job commitments elsewhere); thus, students may find more research and other professional development opportunities in classroom-only versus online programs. The growth of online and hybrid programs and their differences from classroom-only programs begs a more thorough examination of their implications for building student competencies.

Faculty Interests and Expertise

In many master's programs, there may be only three or four faculty available to teach and mentor students in the program. The breadth of faculty interests and expertise can affect what coursework the program can offer based on faculty willingness or comfort with teaching material relevant to the I-O competencies. For example, if faculty have interest and expertise solely in organizational psychology, research methods, and statistics, it will be hard to develop student competencies in employee selection, performance appraisal, and training. Even if faculty members are experienced in these areas, they might not have the freedom in their schedule to cover all the necessary coursework in an area (even if they wanted to) due to other obligations. Part-time faculty may be hired to cover any remaining competencies, but significant time and attention are required to find the right instructors, hire them, and prepare them for teaching in a given program and university. When hiring I-O faculty, it is wise to consider "fit" with the graduate I-O training needs, along with the department's broader expectations for teaching and research.

Faculty interests and expertise also can affect whether and how much they desire to help mentor students in applied experiences. In our experience, some faculty regularly engage in consulting and are happy to include and train graduate students in that work. Other faculty would rather focus on research activities and may not be willing to supervise master's students, particularly if they are already mentoring doctoral students.

Conclusion: A Matrix Tool for Facilitating Program Development

In this chapter we described SIOP's *Guidelines* as they apply to master's programs and discussed a number of options for developing the competencies in the *Guidelines*. We also described how various program characteristics may present opportunities and challenges in addressing the *Guidelines*. Addressing all of these issues as part of a program review or a curriculum redesign effort or in the creation of a new program is a huge undertaking. It would not be surprising if these tasks were viewed as overwhelming or that faculty avoided them entirely because of their scope. Fortunately, a useful tool to facilitate such efforts has been developed and is readily available.

Gibson et al. (2018a) developed an Excel-based matrix template to facilitate this process (available with the *Guidelines* [SIOP, 2016]). The matrix, or curriculum map (Allen, 2004), is designed with the *Guidelines'* 26 competencies listed as rows down the left side. In the columns across the top of the matrix, program faculty can list their courses along with other options they employ to develop student competencies (e.g., internships and other applied experiences, theses and other research, conferences, workshops). Faculty may carefully examine their program offerings and map student opportunities onto the competencies. Gibson et al. noted that a program might simply indicate with an "X" when a class or other experience addresses a competency. A program also could take a more advanced approach, indicating when a class or other option merely introduces a competency area (indicated with an "I"), practices it with feedback ("P"), or offers students the opportunity to demonstrate competence at a mastery level ("D"). Given the diversity among I-O master's programs, the goal of this process likely will not be to demonstrate depth across all 26 competencies. Instead, most programs will probably seek to document a curriculum that generally reflects the *Guidelines* in relation to the program's chosen emphasis.

The first author successfully employed a version of this tool with his program colleagues in a recent examination of their curriculum. Not only did the process allow us to see "missed" areas, but it also revealed places where we were unknowingly duplicating efforts to develop student competence. The process stimulated a lengthy, thoughtful, and rewarding conversation about the opportunities we offer students inside and outside the classroom, and we were able to identify areas we wanted to target with future faculty hires in the program. We hope that the information provided in this chapter provides useful guidance and leads to similarly thoughtful conversations in the reader's program.

References

Allen, M. J. (2004). *Assessing academic programs in higher education*. Boston: Anker Publishing.

American Psychological Association, Board of Educational Affairs. (2004). *Developing and evaluating standards and guidelines related to education and training in psychology: Context, procedures, criteria, and format*. Washington, DC: Author.

Boden, D., Borrego, M., & Newswander, L. K. (2011). Student socialization in interdisciplinary doctoral education. *Higher Education, 62*, 741–755. doi:10.1007/s10734-011-9415-1

Bridle, H., Vrietling, A., Cardillo, M., Araya, Y., & Hinojosa, L. (2013). Preparing for an interdisciplinary future: A perspective from early-career researchers. *Futures, 53*, 22–32. doi.org/10.1016/j.futures.2013.09.003

Francois, E. J. (2014). Motivational orientations of non-traditional adult students to enroll in a degree-seeking program. *New Horizons in Adult Education and Human Resource Development, 26*, 19–35.

Gibson, J. L., Allen, J. A., Payne, S. C., Huelsman, T. J., & Fritsch, A. (2018a). The *Guidelines for Education and Training in Industrial-Organizational Psychology*: 2016/2017 revision and curriculum matrix template. *The Industrial-Organizational Psychologist, 55*(3), 78–81.

Gibson, J. L., Payne, S. C., Morgan, W. B., & Allen, J. A. (2018b). The Society for Industrial and Organizational Psychology's *Guidelines for Education and Training*: An executive summary of the 2016/2017 revision. *American Psychologist, 73*, 678–682.

Payne, S. C., Morgan, W. B., & Allen, J. A. (2015). Revising SIOP's guidelines for education and training: Graduate program director survey results. *The Industrial-Organizational Psychologist, 53*(2), 158–161.

Shoenfelt, E. L., Kottke, J. L., & Stone, N. J. (2012). Master's and undergraduate industrial/organizational internships: Data-based recommendations for successful experiences. *Teaching of Psychology, 39*, 100–106.

Shoenfelt, E. L. Stone, N. J., & Kottke, J. L. (2013). Internships: An established mechanism for increasing employability. *Industrial and Organizational Psychology: Perspectives on Science and Practice, 6*, 24–28.

Society for Industrial and Organizational Psychology, Inc. (2016). *Guidelines for education and training in industrial-organizational psychology*. Bowling Green, OH: Author. https://www.siop.org/Events-Education/Educators/Guidelines-Education-Training

Tett, R. P., Brown, C., & Walser, B. (2014). The 2011 SIOP graduate program benchmarking survey part 7: Thesis, dissertations, and performance expectations. *The Industrial-Organizational Psychologist, 51*(4), 62–73.

Tett, R. P., Brown, C., Walser, B., Simonet, D. V., Davis, J. B., Tonidandel, S., & Hebl, M. (2012). The 2011 SIOP graduate program benchmarking survey: Overview and selected norms. *The Industrial-Organizational Psychologist, 50*(2), 25–38.

Tett, R. P., Brown, C., Walser, B. & Tonidandel, S. (2013). The 2011 SIOP graduate program benchmarking survey part 4: Internships. *The Industrial-Organizational Psychologist, 51*(1), 40–52.

Tett, R. P., Brown, C., Walser, B., Tonidandel, S., & Simonet, D. V. (2013). The 2011 SIOP graduate program benchmarking survey part 5: Comprehensive exams. *The Industrial-Organizational Psychologist, 51*(2), 57–70.

Tett, R., Walser, B., & Brown, C. (2014). The 2011 SIOP graduate program benchmarking survey part 8: Correlations and latent themes. *The Industrial-Organizational Psychologist, 52*(1), 163–176.

Tett, R. P., Walser, B., Brown, C., Tonidandel, S., & Simonet, D. V. (2014). The 2011 SIOP graduate program benchmarking survey part 6: Assistantships, fellowships, and resources. *The Industrial-Organizational Psychologist, 51*(3), 54–57.

4

Importance of Applied Experiences

Course Projects, Practica, Simulations, and Internships

Janet L. Kottke, Kenneth S. Shultz, and Michael G. Aamodt

Introduction

As discussed in Chapter 3 in this volume, the Society for Industrial and Organizational Psychology (SIOP) *Guidelines for Education and Training in Industrial and Organizational Psychology* (2016) take a competency-based approach regarding the proper training of industrial-organizational (I-O) psychologists at both the master's and doctoral level. Although there are distinctions between standalone master's and doctoral education programs in terms of depth and breadth, even given the shorter timeframe of the former, the core competencies to be acquired remain largely the same. The SIOP *Guidelines* focus heavily on knowledge acquisition in the core areas of I-O psychology, fields of psychology, history and systems, ethical and legal issues, as well as research methods and statistics knowledge. As Byrne, Hayes, McPhail, Hakel, Cortina, and McHenry (2014) noted, the *Guidelines* are more curriculum focused than competency focused.

In this chapter, we emphasize the development of professional skills (e.g., project management and consulting skills) within the context of curriculum. These competencies are most commonly developed by completing internships (Shoenfelt, Kottke, & Stone, 2012; Shoenfelt, Stone, & Kottke, 2013), working on applied class projects, and engaging in practicum projects (Kottke, Olson, & Shultz, 2016). Throughout this chapter, we offer examples of applied projects. These projects range from the foundational (job analysis and training) to the novel (an assessment center staffed by master's I-O graduate students). Our objective is to offer the reader illustrative and interesting applications for use within the master's I-O curriculum.

Janet L. Kottke, Kenneth S. Shultz, and Michael G. Aamodt, *Importance of Applied Experiences* In: *Mastering Industrial-Organizational Psychology*. Edited by: Elizabeth L. Shoenfelt, Oxford University Press (2020). © Society for Industrial and Organizational Psychology. DOI: 10.1093/oso/9780190071141.003.0004.

The Value of Applications for Students and Faculty

Professional competencies are often identified as a distinguishing feature for entry-level success in the field of I-O psychology (Zelin, Lider, Doverspike, Oliver, & Trusty, 2014). A recent survey (Shoenfelt, 2019a) of 143 employers of I-O terminal master's graduates revealed that when asked, "What differentiates an average applicant from a superior applicant?" employers identified professional competencies such as "communication skills" (68%), "attitude" (66%), "work ethic" (59%), "interpersonal skills" (55%), "experience" (42%), and "business savvy/acumen" (40%). "Technical knowledge" (43%) and "research skills" (27%) rounded out the skills assessed.

A parallel survey (Shoenfelt, 2019b) of 958 graduates of terminal master's programs asked them to "Select up to 3 of the most useful [faculty activities] in preparing you for your career after graduate school." The most popular response, by almost double any other, was the activity "Included applied I-O projects as a part of coursework" (62%). The next most popular response was "Provided opportunities to participate in I-O projects in/for organizations [outside of class; paid or unpaid]" (37%). "Encouraged I-O internships" (31%), "Provided access to I-O internships" (17%), and "Supported students in obtaining I-O internships" (16%) had an impressive combined 64% of respondents endorsing internships as most useful in preparing them for their careers after graduate school. Clearly, students value the applied work offered in their programs.

Scientist-Practitioner Model as the Basis for Applications Within I-O Training

Space limitations do not permit a thorough review of the now-considerable literature that presents issues surrounding the application of the scientist-practitioner (S-P) model (cf. Ones, Kaiser, Chamorro-Premuzic, & Svensson, 2017; Rupp & Beal, 2007). In sum, this debate manifests itself as concern about the gap between science and practice—that academics are too focused on theory building, thus not addressing practitioner needs, and practitioners are too willing to implement organizational programs without empirical evidence for their effectiveness. As faculty in master's programs, we are essentially on the front lines of this debate—our students will typically enter practitioner roles upon graduation. With that in mind, though other models have been suggested as frameworks-in-use for training I-O psychologists (cf. Hays-Thomas, 2006), the S-P model has persisted as an ideal (Zickar & Gibby, 2007) and can be found embodied in the aforementioned guidelines for training by SIOP.

So that readers are aware of our preferences, we subscribe to the tenets of the S-P model: We take as a fundamental principle that the S-P model serves as an admirable guiding framework for our decision making as I-O psychologists. The S-P model guides us as we consider what kind of exercises, class projects, and practical experiences to implement within our programs. We believe students should learn first the empirical literature and then be given opportunities to apply this knowledge to organizational settings. This chapter is the result of our many years of implementing practical applications that solidify students' developing knowledge of the field.

Student Benefits: Development of Employable Skillsets

As was seen in the employer survey (Shoenfelt, 2019a), employers especially value communication, attitude, work ethic, and experience in master's graduates. These results complement national surveys in which employers of college graduates stress the importance of critical thinking, collaboration in teams, and professionalism in employees (Casillas, Kyllonen, & Way, 2019), which are competencies inherent in practical experiences. Further, practical experiences develop student skills that improve employability (Kottke, Shoenfelt, & Stone, 2014). Shoenfelt et al. (2012), for example, found that several skills rated by employers (e.g., work ethic, professionalism, organizational savvy) were enhanced through applied experience (i.e., an internship).

Faculty Benefits: Putting the Practitioner into Scientist-Practitioner

Although a key objective of this chapter is to provide readers ideas about how to incorporate practical experiences for students into their classes and programs, we would be remiss if we did not note the benefits of practical experiences that accrue to faculty and programs. As educators of future practitioners, it is important to keep our "saws" sharp. By working with organizations and other applied professionals to provide practical experiences for students, we apply research knowledge to organizational settings. In turn, this work with organizations informs our research. Relevant questions can be addressed in faculty and student research,[1] and these organization–program partnerships may lead to sites for data collection (Shoenfelt, Stone, & Kottke, 2018). To be sure, these are not likely the intended objectives of these organizational contacts. Nonetheless, these partnerships form a very valuable feedback loop for faculty. Furthermore, at standalone I-O programs in which the publication threshold for faculty is usually lower than for doctoral programs, applied projects may be treated as comparable professional outputs to publications. Finally, many of these projects have considerable benefits to the organizations served and enhance the reputation of the graduate programs involved.

Applied Projects

General Considerations

As noted at the beginning of this chapter, whereas the core professional competencies that lead to the success of applied (i.e., non-academic) master's- and doctoral-level I-O psychologists are largely the same, the development of those competencies can be diverse given the inherent differences in master's versus doctoral training programs. Doctoral programs frequently fund their students with teaching and research assistantships or fellowships and often have smaller cohorts each year than do terminal master's-level programs. Most noteworthy, master's programs are typically two years in length, but the typical doctoral program is four to six years in length (for those entering with a BA degree).

There are more than 185 I-O master's programs listed on the SIOP website. The programs' websites list a dizzying array of courses, as well as other graduation requirements. For example, some master's programs have a formal practicum course, while others do not. Whereas some I-O master's programs require a master's thesis, others offer the options of completing a thesis,

---

[1] Although there is debate about the value of completing a thesis if the student will be seeking employment immediately upon graduation (cf. Erffmeyer & Mendel, 1990), the thesis serves as a notable example of project management. The student must manage a committee of faculty, identify the proper site to collect data, write a significant and very technical report (the thesis), and do this within a compressed timeframe. In short, these experiences mirror many aspects of the types of work that students engage in upon graduation (Shultz & Kottke, 1997). Please also see Chapter 5 in this volume.

capstone project, or comprehensive exam. Still other programs may offer the option of developing a portfolio that combines aspects of each component as their culminating experience for the degree. Some master's programs may require an internship, while others may only encourage or even discourage an internship. These dynamic curriculum differences can have important implications for how students develop practical professional competencies through applied experiences within their training program. As noted in the SIOP *Guidelines*, students can develop professional skills in a multitude of ways, from projects and assignments in formal coursework, to supervised field experiences either through a practicum course, internship, or working with faculty on pro bono or paid consulting projects.

In addition, some standalone I-O master's programs emphasize applied versus a more balanced S-P approach to training students. Thus, the program's emphasis will afford students distinct opportunities to develop professional competencies. Although we emphasize in this chapter the importance of applied experiences via a wide variety of options to I-O master's students, doing so should not be to the detriment of instilling the S-P model that has traditionally distinguished I-O psychology training from related fields such as human resources (HR) and organizational behavior (Aamodt, 2016).

Faculty Preparation, Experience, and Contacts

For faculty members to supervise master's students in enriching applied experiences, we must be up to date on current best practices in the field of applied I-O psychology. This can be accomplished by working with applied I-O colleagues on projects, attending workshops and annual professional conferences in the field of I-O psychology, and reading relevant professional literature. Faculty members in I-O master's programs can remain current and gain experience by also engaging in pro bono and/or paid consulting projects. These projects may or may not include students, depending on the level of expertise needed in the applied consulting projects.

Student Preparation

For meaningful engagement in applied I-O related projects, students must first develop core I-O knowledge and skills (Kottke et al., 2016). It would not make sense to have students engage in large-scale organizational interventions in their first term in a master's program. Instead, master's students can begin to systematically develop the fundamental knowledge and skills outlined in the SIOP *Guidelines* through class projects, simulations, case studies, and similar activities. For example, students in the first two authors' I-O program take a performance management class in their first term where they complete, in teams, job analysis projects. Thus, students begin to develop critical oral, written, and interpersonal communication skills while working on a limited-scope project during the first term in their master's program.

Developing Organizational Partnerships

Potential "Clients"

There are a wide variety of potential "clients" for applied projects, regardless of the geographical location of the I-O master's program (cf. Shoenfelt, 2003). For example, although there are I-O master's programs in small towns and rural areas, students are able to complete applied projects with small and medium-sized companies, as well as with nonprofits and government agencies such as town and county governments, school systems, police departments, hospitals, regional jails, retirement homes, and credit unions. Thus, applied projects are not limited to programs in large cities with access to large organizations.

Organizational Entry, Relationship Building, Contracting

There are many ways to gain access to organizations. Usually this access is the result of relationships that faculty have developed with local HR professionals and former students (Shoenfelt et al., 2018), but could also be worksites of friends and neighbors or student connections to current or former employers (O'Neill & Jelley, 2014). For new faculty, however, "cold calls" to organizations can yield successful results. For example, an initial call to the town manager, police chief, or school principal typically results in an initial meeting to discuss potential projects. During this meeting, the I-O faculty member should explain the field of I-O psychology (Shoenfelt et al., 2018) and indicate the types of projects students could complete, such as conducting job analyses or developing performance appraisal systems, compensation systems, training programs, or structured interviews. The third author recalls only one time in 25+ years of teaching that a public official failed to express an interest in a potential project. The success rate with cold calls to private organizations has been lower. As a faculty member gains experience and develops a larger professional network, cold calls are seldom needed.

Another way to establish potential clients for applied projects is to join local chapters of professional organizations such as the Society for Human Resource Management (SHRM; https://www.shrm.org), Association for Talent Development (https://www.td.org; formerly American Society for Training and Development), Industry Liaison Group (http://www.nationalilg.org), Personnel Testing Councils, and local I-O networking groups. Although Industry Liaison Group and Personnel Testing Councils chapters are found only in larger cities, SHRM chapters can be found virtually everywhere. Finding clients through these organizations can take time to develop contacts. Although not impossible, appearing at one meeting and requesting a project site is not likely to be successful. Instead, it is important to establish a personal relationship with the chapter members before seeking their help. Some I-O faculty have found great success in establishing partnerships with local SHRM chapters by attending meetings and becoming involved in committees. Participating in chapter committees is especially important to effectively build relationships through extended contact.

Finally, consider working with one's university. Aside from the fact that most universities are complex systems with significant opportunities in which to practice I-O craft, in most cases, the university will also be very supportive of student projects. For example, one master's program established a partnership with the university's residential life program to develop and improve existing processes to hire, evaluate, and train residential life staff. Because these projects can be completed during evening hours, this partnership works well for the graduate students, most of whom are working adults who complete a substantial portion of their coursework online.

Projects and Activities Within Courses

In this section, we describe applied projects within courses. Because of space limitations, we limit our discussion to a few examples and mention key considerations in conducting these activities. Some projects are fundamental, straightforward applications (e.g., job analysis) while others may be less often employed yet equally impactful for organizations (e.g., salary surveys).

Applied Projects

Job Analysis

Because job analysis results serve as the basis for many I-O psychology activities (Aamodt, 2016), it is important that I-O graduate students get experience in conducting them and writing job descriptions. Job analysis need not be a complicated class project. Students can write a job description of a position they would like to hold. Alternatively, they can interview each other in the class about jobs they have held and then write a job description based on that interview (cf. Kottke, 1988). However, this simple interview does not provide the opportunity to perform other job analysis activities such as observing job performance, conducting focus groups, or administering task inventories. Nor does it allow the student to experience some of the practical difficulties (e.g., scheduling, finding a place to interview, language barriers) associated with an actual job analysis.

Finding sites for job analysis usually is not difficult. Over the years, students at the third author's I-O program have conducted job analysis interviews and observations for town governments and school systems, and task analyses for law enforcement agencies. The goal of these projects was to provide the agencies with thorough job descriptions (usually about five pages long), which they could use as the basis for subsequent personnel functions.

The class has an initial meeting with the agency point of contact (POC), usually the HR director, to discuss the project, understand the nature of the agency, and determine logistics for the observations and interviews. Essential to project success is that the POC notifies agency employees to explain the nature of the project and to ask for their cooperation. Once observations and interviews are conducted, students write job descriptions, which are reviewed by other students before instructor review and feedback is provided for revisions to develop the final job descriptions, which are then delivered to the POC.

Training Program Development and Delivery

Many I-O master's programs offer courses in employee training (Tett, Walser, Brown, Simonet, & Tonidandel, 2013); in fact, training was ranked high in surveys of the competences required for jobs acquired by master's students (Trahan & McAllister, 2002). In training courses, students often are given the opportunity not only to develop a training program, but to deliver it. Presenting multiple sessions of the same training provides an opportunity to improve skills with each session. Training delivery occurs in the last few weeks of the term, after students learn course content, develop their training program, and practice delivery. This can be a busy time for the instructor, who attends each practice and training session and may be called upon to respond to "out of scope" questions beyond the students' expertise.

Colleagues have indicated they have used a variety of training audiences, including fellow class members, company employees, SHRM members at a monthly chapter meeting, university employees, and employees from several organizations that came to a central location for training. A non-student audience greatly enhances the experience for students as they must prepare for "on the ground" questions from a motivated audience.

The topic for the training program must be one in which the students have more expertise than the audience. Most likely these will be "technical" topics such as creating a structured interview or evaluating a selection test battery. Performance appraisal is an example of a topic that could be both appropriate and inappropriate for a given audience. Training focused on how to develop a job-related performance appraisal scale might be of interest to HR professionals, who likely are better informed than students on how to provide performance feedback.

A training program on a specific company policy often works well for this assignment. In one such project, the students provided training to county employees on the county's harassment policy. Because it was a new policy, none of the employees had prior knowledge. Students spent considerable time learning the policy, asking the HR director questions, and developing an interactive training program.

Another illustrative class project was training provided to about 50 supervisors from various local law enforcement agencies on the overtime provisions of the Fair Labor Standards Act. This opportunity arose from several publicized complaints that local law enforcement agencies were not properly compensating their officers for on-call time and meal breaks. This topic had been covered extensively in a prior course and students were well prepared to develop targeted training. A local attorney and SHRM member volunteered to ensure that the students accurately answered any legal questions from the audience.

Structured Interview Developments

Occasionally, organizational needs present learning opportunities that span more than one course. For example, the development of a structured interview can be assigned in a training or selection course, or both. Structured interviews are more valid predictors and are more likely to withstand legal scrutiny than are unstructured interviews (e.g., Alonso, Moscoso, & Salgado, 2017). Thus, teaching students how to develop structured interviews in an applied setting is especially desirable, particularly if job analysis and competency data are already available. If these data are not available, focus groups can be used to generate competencies.

For one such project, the third author recruited organizations his I-O program had worked with previously: a local SHRM chapter, two police departments, and local government agencies. During the morning session of a full-day training, I-O students presented the basics of structured interviewing and employment law. In the afternoon, students met separately with members of each organization to identify the competencies suitable for a structured interview and began writing potential interview questions and scoring protocols. Students had to use considerable tact when reviewing the clients' current interview questions, most of which were not job related and some of which were potentially illegal. Following the full-day training, the students worked with the organization over the next month to finalize the interview. This activity provided the students with two résumé entries, conducting a training program and developing a structured interview.

Salary Surveys

Although compensation is not a topic commonly taught in I-O graduate programs, especially doctoral programs (Tett et al., 2013), it is an area in which I-O master's graduates find jobs. For many years, one I-O program partnered with the local SHRM chapter to conduct an annual salary and benefits survey. The job titles included in the survey were chosen by the SHRM chapter. Respondents provided salary information for each title as well as information about the organization's employee benefits (e.g., sick days, insurance, retirement contributions). The chapter promoted the survey to chapter members. I-O master's students analyzed the data via Excel and created a technical report summarizing the results, including Excel-generated tables. This experience with Excel supplemented the SPSS skills the students had already acquired. In addition, students were exposed to a hands-on application of the importance of data cleaning. For example, one respondent indicated employees received 180 days of paid sick leave each year; another reported salaries for several jobs that were below the legal minimum wage. Identifying these data issues required students to apply critical thinking and gain experience contacting employers to clarify responses.

Simulations

Interview as Final Exam

Kottke, Valencia, and Shultz (2013) described a panel interview as the culminating experience for a first-year master's personnel selection class. The interview panel typically consists of either two faculty members or the faculty member currently teaching the class and two second-year I-O master's students. Students "apply" for an internship at a local (but fictitious) consulting firm. The 15-minute individual interview sessions are an authentic role-play. Students take the interview seriously and fully engage with the scenario (interview scores count for 15% to 20% of the final grade). An important follow-up to the interview is a reflection paper where students discuss both their preparation for and reactions to the interview. Reflection papers are widely used, especially for internships (Bailey, Barber, & Nelson, 2017; Barber & Bailey, 2015) and, within this context, help to link course concepts with student experiences. In these papers, students often comment on the realism of the interview and how it helped them prepare for their internship interviews.

Performance Coaching Session as Final Exam

The second author has used a simulated coaching session as a final exam for his graduate performance management class. Students are provided a scenario describing two subordinates at different career stages, facing unique performance issues. Students prepare for a 15-minute individual coaching session, with the faculty member role-playing a first-line supervisor in need of coaching. Students provide specific coaching recommendations to the supervisor regarding how to handle the two specific subordinates described in the scenario. Students also are asked to briefly describe best practices and current issues in performance management to help the manager better improve the organization's existing performance management process.

Courses Designed for Applied Experiences

Practica

As can be seen from these examples of class projects, master's students can be engaged in hands-on activities that accentuate fundamental aspects of I-O training. Some programs designate courses as practica in which students are concurrently enrolled in a course for university credit and placed on a job site to perform work under the supervision of a professional. As a testament to their use within master's programs, 53% of the respondents to a recent graduate survey (Shoenfelt, 2019b) had completed a practicum. These courses are important for the development of the I-O students. In this section, we describe projects suitable for practicum projects and make recommendations for conducting these courses.

Appropriate Projects

The types of potential projects for an applied practicum course are nearly infinite, encompassing the full range of I-O applications. For novice practicum instructors, we recommend initial projects be standard fare, such as job analyses, for organizations with whom you may be familiar. Particularly fruitful job sites are likely to be found where alumni of the program or other professionals knowledgeable about I-O psychology work (Shoenfelt, 2003; Shoenfelt et al., 2018). A good starting place may be projects for your university. For example, the second author contacted the associate vice president of human resources (AVP-HR) to discuss possible applied projects. The AVP-HR wished to create web-based versions of exempt and nonexempt employee hard-copy performance appraisal forms to increase ease of use, reduce redundancy, and increase the effectiveness of the existing forms. The AVP-HR and her team came to an early class session and presented her ideas for updating and automating the paper forms. Following the meeting, the practicum class split into two project teams, one working with exempt employees and the other with nonexempt employees. The teams interviewed subject matter experts individually and in focus groups to update and automate the existing performance appraisal form, creating a web-based version for each respective employee group. A final technical report with recommendations and examples was created, along with a summary presentation made to the AVP-HR and her team, all within a 10-week term. This applied project was incredibly impactful and the forms are still used, a decade later, by all university staff employees.

Because students are apprentices, projects should be vetted carefully in advance of the course start date (cf. Troper & Lopez, 2009). It is important to be flexible and have a "plan B" in mind as projects sometimes fall through at the last minute (cf. O'Neill & Jelley, 2014). It is also important to know your organizational contacts, structural features of the organization, skillsets of the students, and your availability for out-of-class meetings associated with the project.

No matter the preparation, events beyond your control may require midcourse adjustments. For this very reason, it is vital to prepare students attitudinally for such eventualities. In a notable case, the first author had lined up a job analysis project with a local school district. The director of the HR division had indicated that several job descriptions were stale, requiring updates. This type of project is ideal for first-year I-O students as it is finite in scope and takes advantage of knowledge learned in earlier classes. The HR director and associate director came to the first class meeting and briefly demonstrated the software to be used to collect the job analysis data. The first hiccup came a week later when the instructor scheduled the visit to the school district headquarters. In the intervening week, the school board had relieved the HR director of his job and the associate director was now interim director. Nonetheless, the project was to go ahead, and a time was set to meet with job incumbents. When the instructor and students arrived to conduct a half-day of interviews, they discovered job incumbents had been told nothing about the interviews, other than a directive to meet with an outside group. Given the surrounding upheaval, the job incumbents were leery of the students—they feared for their jobs. The students took the turmoil in good stride, and in the final analysis, they learned a great deal about the importance of communicating the purposes for job analyses and how critical the need is for support of all organizational constituents. Though the firing of the HR director probably could not have been foreseen, the lessons from this project remind us to ask a host of questions in advance about the organization and to prepare students to expect challenges.

Range of Projects Possible

For the annual applied practicum course taught by the first two authors, students have conducted many job analyses, created structured interview protocols, and developed performance appraisal instruments (Kottke et al., 2016). Other, less common, projects have included organizational culture assessment and analysis of recruitment strategies for law enforcement.

Instructors should not feel confined to traditional I-O topics. For example, the first author was contacted by the director of a local nonprofit that operates programs for infants and children (aged zero to five) and their parents. The question that had vexed the director was why breastfeeding rates were so much lower in her county than in an adjacent county that had very similar educational levels and nationally funded resources for new mothers. To uncover the answer, the students drew upon their prior coursework in research methods, data collection techniques and analysis, organizational development, and needs assessment. Though this project was not a typical I-O project, it helped students to exercise critical thinking and appreciate the impact I-O projects can have in a wide variety of organizational settings and topics.

Concomitant Development and Assessment (via an Assessment Center) of Professional Skills

Assessment centers (ACs) have been used for some time to select and develop leaders (Gaugler, Rosenthal, Thornton, & Bentson, 1987; Hoffman, Kennedy, LoPilato, Monahan, & Lance, 2015). ACs have a more recent history of use in education for development and outcome assessment (Riggio, Mayes, & Schleicher, 2003). Kottke and Shultz (1997) described an AC that provided practicum students feedback about skills traditionally assessed in ACs. Students in the practicum underwent a full day of exercises (in-basket, role-play, leaderless group discussion, oral presentation) and were assessed on their written and oral communication, problem-solving, interpersonal, organizing (time management), and organizational survival skills. Students gained exposure to a type of assessment commonly used for developmental feedback—feedback that has been shown to support self-efficacy for improvement, which in turn leads to better performance and more promotions (Dimotakis, Mitchell, & Maurer, 2017). Additionally, second-year students gained practice as assessors, which gave them an advantage when assessors were sought both locally and nationally. Although a full-scale AC may be impractical for long-term use without a substantial investment of time, introducing these types of exercises into the curriculum offers students valuable experience and future career benefits.

Internships

Internships are widely used (Binder, Baguley, Crook, & Miller, 2015) and have been defined as "structured and career relevant work experiences obtained by students prior to graduation from an academic program" (Taylor, 1988, p. 393). Internships are differentiated from employment, whether short term or permanent, by the intention that certain learning objectives will be met by the experience. Through a well-managed internship, students encounter the expectations of the work world, ease the transition into their future jobs, and increase their job options. Internships may be of increased importance to I-O master's students because many seek applied employment immediately upon graduation. No doubt this is one reason that the *Guidelines* (SIOP, 2016) highly recommend internships. In fact, a recent graduate survey (Shoenfelt, 2019b) revealed that only 19% of master's students had not completed an internship. It appears the message has been received.

Many of the suggestions already made about other applied experiences apply to internships as well. Here, our goal is to make specific suggestions so the internship yields the intended results (Bailey et al., 2017; Knouse & Fontenot, 2008; Kottke & Shultz, 2002; Shoenfelt et al., 2012).

Site Host Responsibilities

First and foremost, there needs to be adequate on-site supervision. Adequate supervisor support (D'Abate, 2010; McHugh, 2017) is an important predictor of internship efficacy. Without supervisor support, it is difficult for students to apply the knowledge they have acquired in their coursework—and the organization also will suffer from lost opportunities. Supervisors need to understand the objective of the internship is to engage the student in a learning experience, not to use the student as an economical alternative to an employee. Because the student is a representative of the campus program and independent of the campus oversight inherent in class projects or practica, students need to understand their responsibilities. This ethos is built upon strong content knowledge and an attitude of accountability prior to being sent to a host organization (Shoenfelt et al., 2012).

On-Campus Coordination

On-campus coordination is critical to ensure that the student and the host organization have clear shared expectations of the purpose of the internship and are able to carry out their respective obligations. Once an organization has become a host for interns, it is important that there be a feedback loop so the interns acquire the experience they desire and the host obtains quality interns.

As a suitable example of a structure for closing feedback loops, one program's internship director is responsible for overseeing the internship program, keeping track of the various host sites, and updating the internship manual.[2] The director reviews the student applications for internship placements. In these proposals, students describe the aims and goals they have for their internships. After students are matched to an internship site, the on-site supervisor is not only responsible for providing guidance and feedback for the student while on site, but ultimately conducts a performance appraisal of the student, submitted to the internship director. Interns submit a final report of the experience to the internship director and complete an exit survey. Both the student reports and the exit survey serve as feedback loops to the program to be certain that the internship site met the expectations of the program and to determine if an organization is suitable to continue to host internships.

The internship may be the single most important applied experience that students receive in their programs. The literature is clear that the internship can be transformational in a student's career. Often, students obtain their first professional jobs at their internship sites (Zhao & Liden, 2011). A recent graduate survey (Shoenfelt, 2019ab) echoed these findings: 30% of the respondents reported their first professional jobs came from their internship sites, 79% agreed or strongly agreed that the internship had prepared them for their jobs, and 64% agreed or strongly agreed that the internship had helped define their career paths. In addition, data from the graduate survey indicated that those who had completed an internship spent less time searching for a job.[3] Taken together, these data underscore the importance of implementing and monitoring quality internship placements for master's-level I-O programs.

---

[2] The program referenced has an internship manual in which the responsibilities of the host supervisor and student are laid out.

[3] Using data from a graduate survey (Shoenfelt, 2019b), a cross-tabulation of the responses to the question ". . . did you complete one or more internships?" with ". . . how long did it take for you to secure your first professional I-O position?" found a weak, negative relationship. If a nominal variable for having completed an internship (or not) is used, the relationship between it and length of time to obtain first professional position is −.07 (point-biserial). If responses are treated as an ordinal variable, ranging from no internship through unpaid to paid internship, the relationship is −.16 (Spearman rho, $N = 861$).

Evidence for Experiential Learning Linking
to Job Performance

As I-O psychologists, we "know" that practical experience is important for our students, but do we have data-driven evidence? Yes and no. Most data appear program specific (Rothman & Sisman, 2016; Rowe, 2015), and very little research has specifically examined master's I-O students or graduates.[4] When we turn to the literature beyond I-O, we find that experiential education goes by many labels (e.g., work-integrated learning, co-op learning, internships), making it difficult to find an integrated or definitive literature of its effectiveness.

The most defined data-driven literature appears to be for internships. As has already been mentioned, internships increase students' professional, interpersonal, technical, and presentation skills (Shoenfelt et al., 2012). Internships solidify for students their career interests (Rothman & Sissman, 2016), often serve as their first professional jobs (Shoenfelt, 2019b; Zhao & Liden, 2011), and may reduce the time searching for the first professional job (Inceoglu, Selenko, McDowall, & Schlachter, 2018; Shoenfelt, 2019b). Finally, there is emerging evidence that internships have an impact on self-identity (Inceoglu et al., 2018).

Empirical evidence for the benefits of practica is more elusive. The best evidence may come from proxies for applied experiences. One such proxy is the evidence for ACs that are used while students are still in college. Data-driven evidence has emerged that suggests merely being exposed to the AC method has benefits as students use the exposure as a springboard to seek additional feedback from others (Extejt, Forbes, & Smith, 1996). These effects may extend into students' first jobs. Two studies have found that AC skills assessed as an undergraduate predicted career trajectory two or more years after graduation (Riggio et al., 2003; Waldman & Korbar, 2004).

Finally, turning to the evidence for applied class projects, we find support for student learning in the broader literature of problem-based instruction. In their meta-analysis comparing conventional to problem-based instruction, Dochy, Segers, Van den Bossche, and Gijbels (2003) found consistently large effect sizes for skill acquisition that persisted beyond graduation. Prince (2004) found comparable results in a systematic review of meta-analyses

---

[4] Shoenfelt et al. (2012) is a notable exception. These authors assessed employers' views of the skillsets of I-O master's students before and after an internship.

that addressed cooperative and collaborative, in addition to problem-based, learning. Taken together, these results support employing the kinds of project that have been highlighted in this chapter.

Summary and Conclusions

In this chapter, we have provided an overview of practical experiences for master's I-O students. We have described course projects, simulations, practica, and internships as exemplars of applied experiences. In addition, we have offered guidance on the prerequisites of faculty preparation, community partnerships, and student readiness to undertake these projects. Finally, we have given a brief overview of the data-driven evidence for applied experiences. We hope that this chapter will inspire I-O instructors affiliated with master's programs to adopt, adapt, and create from these ideas their own experiential projects for their students.

References

Aamodt, M. (2016). *Industrial/organizational psychology: An applied approach* (8th ed., Chapters 1, 2). Boston: Cengage Learning.

Alonso, P., Moscoso, S., & Salgado, J. F. (2017). Structured behavioral interview as a legal guarantee for ensuring equal employment opportunities for women: A meta-analysis. *European Journal of Psychology Applied to Legal Context, 9*(1), 15–23. https://doi.org/10.1016/j.ejpal.2016.03.002

Bailey, S. F., Barber, L. K., & Nelson, V. L. (2017). Undergraduate internship supervision in psychology departments: Use of experiential learning best practices. *Psychology Learning & Teaching, 16*(1), 74–83. https://doi.org/10.1177/1475725716671234

Barber, L. K., & Bailey, S. F. (2015). *Internship resources for developing student employability*. Davidson, NC: Office of Teaching Resources in Psychology. http://teachpsych.org/Resources/Documents/otrp/resources/barber14.pdf

Binder, J. F., Baguley, T., Crook, C., & Miller, F. (2015). The academic value of internships: Benefits across disciplines and student backgrounds. *Contemporary Educational Psychology, 41*, 73–82. https://doi.org/10.1016/j.cedpsych.2014.12.001

Byrne, Z. S., Hayes, T. L., McPhail, S. M., Hakel, M. D., Cortina, J. M., & McHenry, J. J. (2014). Educating I-O psychologists for science and practice: Where do we go from here? *Industrial and Organizational Psychology: Perspectives on Science and Practice, 7*(1), 2–14. https://doi.org/10.1111/iops.12095

Casillas, A., Kyllonen, P. C., & Way, J. (2019). Preparing students for the future of work: A formative assessment approach. In F. Oswald, T. S. Behrend, & L. Foster (Eds.), *Workforce readiness and the future of work* (Chapter 3). New York: Routledge. https://doi.org/10.4324/9781351210485-3

D'Abate, C. (2010). Developmental interactions for business students: Do they make a difference? *Journal of Leadership & Organizational Studies, 17*(2), 143–155. https://doi.org/10.1177/1548051810370795

Dimotakis, N., Mitchell, D., & Maurer, T. (2017). Positive and negative assessment center feedback in relation to development self-efficacy, feedback seeking, and promotion. *Journal of Applied Psychology, 102*(11), 1514–1527. doi:http://dx.doi.org/10.1037/apl0000228

Dochy, F., Segers, M., Van den Bossche, P., & Gijbels, D. (2003). Effects of problem-based learning: A meta-analysis. *Learning and Instruction, 13*(5), 533–568. https://doi.org/10.1016/S0959-4752(02)00025-7

Erffmeyer, E. S., & Mendel, R. M. (1990). Master's level training in industrial/organizational psychology: A case study of the perceived relevance of graduate training. *Professional Psychology: Research and Practice, 21*(5), 405–408. http://dx.doi.org/10.1037/0735-7028.21.5.405

Extejt, M. M., Forbes, J. B., & Smith, J. E. (1996). Evaluation of a multimethod undergraduate management skills development program. *Journal of Education for Business, 71*(4), 223–231. https://doi.org/10.1080/08832323.1996.10116789

Gaugler, B. B., Rosenthal, D. B., Thornton, G. C., & Bentson, C. (1987). Meta-analysis of assessment center validity. *Journal of Applied Psychology, 72*(3), 493–511. https://doi.org/10.1037/0021-9010.72.3.493

Hays-Thomas, R. (2006). Challenging the scientist-practitioner model: Questions about IO education and training. *The Industrial-Organizational Psychologist, 44*(1), 47–53. https://doi.org/10.1037/e579122011-006

Hoffman, B. J., Kennedy, C. L., LoPilato, A. C., Monahan, E. L., & Lance, C. E. (2015). A review of the content, criterion-related, and construct-related validity of assessment center exercises. *Journal of Applied Psychology, 100*(4), 1143–1168. doi:http://dx.doi.org/10.1037/a0038707

Inceoglu, I., Selenko, E., McDowall, A., & Schlachter, S. (2018). (How) Do work placements work? Scrutinizing the quantitative evidence for a theory-driven future research agenda. *Journal of Vocational Behavior, 110*, 317–337. https://doi.org/10.1016/j.jvb.2018.09.002

Knouse, S. B., & Fontenot, G. (2008). Benefits of the business college internship: A research review. *Journal of Employment Counseling, 45*(2), 61–66. https://doi.org/10.1002/j.2161-1920.2008.tb00045.x

Kottke, J. L. (1988). A job analysis exercise for an undergraduate industrial psychology class. *Teaching of Psychology, 15*(1), 41–42. ttps://doi.org/10.1207/s15328023top1501_11

Kottke, J. L., Olson, D. A., & Shultz, K. S. (2016). Use of practicum classes to solidify the scientist-practitioner model in master's level training. In C. Wankel & L. Wankel (Eds.), *Integrating curricular and co-curricular endeavors to enhance student outcomes* (Chapter 2, pp. 15–41). Bingley, UK: Emerald Publishing Group. https://doi.org/10.1108/978-1-78635-064-020161002

Kottke, J. L., Shoenfelt, E. L., & Stone, N. J. (2014). Educating industrial–organizational psychologists: Lessons learned from master's programs. *Industrial and Organizational Psychology, 7*(1), 26–31. https://doi.org/10.1111/iops.12099

Kottke, J. L., & Shultz, K. S. (1997). Using an assessment center as a developmental tool for graduate students: A demonstration. *Journal of Social Behavior and Personality, 12*, 289–302.

Kottke, J. L., & Shultz, K. S. (2002, August). Developing, maintaining, and supervising graduate student internships. In N. J. Stone (Chair), *Strategies for teaching I/O psychology*. Symposium presented at the 110th annual convention of the American Psychological Association, Chicago.

Kottke, J. L., Valencia, L. A., & Shultz, K. S. (2013). Using a simulated selection interview as a final examination in a graduate personnel selection class. *Psychology Learning and Teaching, 12*, 290–296. doi:dx.doi.org/10.2304.plat.2013.12.3.290

McHugh, P. P. (2017). The impact of compensation, supervision and work design on internship efficacy: Implications for educators, employers and prospective interns. *Journal of Education and Work, 30*(4), 367–382. https://doi.org/10.1080/13639080.2016.1181729

O'Neill, T. A., & Jelley, R. B. (2014). Integrating practical experiences in I-O courses. *The Industrial-Organizational Psychologist, 52*(1), 142–153.

Ones, D. S., Kaiser, R. B., Chamorro-Premuzic, T., & Svensson, C. (2017). Has industrial-organizational psychology lost its way? *The Industrial-Organizational Psychologist, 54*(4), 67–74.

Prince, M. (2004). Does active learning work? A review of the research. *Journal of Engineering Education, 93*(3), 223–231. https://doi.org/10.1002/j.2168-9830.2004.tb00809.x

Riggio, R. E., Mayes, B. T., & Schleicher, D. J. (2003). Using assessment center methods for measuring undergraduate business student outcomes. *Journal of Management Inquiry, 12*(1), 68–78. https://doi.org/10.1177/1056492602250519

Rowe, P. M. (2015). Researchers' reflections on what is missing from work-integrated learning research. *Asia-Pacific Journal of Cooperative Education, 16*(2), 101–107.

Rothman, M., & Sisman, R. (2016). Internship impact on career consideration among business students. *Education + Training, 58*(9), 1003–1013. https://doi.org/10.1108/ET-04-2015-0027

Rupp, D. E., & Beal, D. (2007). Checking in with the scientist-practitioner model: How are we doing. *The Industrial-Organizational Psychologist, 45*(1), 35–40. https://doi.org/10.1037/e579082011-003

Shoenfelt, E. L. (2003, October). Utilizing applied projects in I-O graduate training: A checklist to help ensure successful experiences. *The Industrial-Organizational Psychologist, 41*(2), 109–115. https://doi.org/10.1037/e578802011-016

Shoenfelt, E. L. (2019a). I-O master's employer survey. Survey conducted for E. L. Shoenfelt (Ed.) (in press), *Mastering the job market: Career issues for master's-level industrial-organizational psychologist*. New York: Oxford University Press.

Shoenfelt, E. L. (2019b). I-O master's graduate survey. Survey conducted for E. L. Shoenfelt (Ed.) (in press), *Mastering the job market: Career issues for master's-level industrial-organizational psychologist*. New York: Oxford University Press.

Shoenfelt, E. L., Kottke, J. L., & Stone, N. J. (2012). Master's and undergraduate industrial/organizational internships: Data-based recommendations for successful experiences. *Teaching of Psychology, 39*(2), 100–106. https://doi.org/10.1177/0098628312437724

Shoenfelt, E. L., Stone, N. J., & Kottke, J. L. (2013). Internships: An established mechanism for increasing employability. *Industrial and Organizational Psychology, 6*(1), 24–27. https://doi.org/10.1111/iops.12004

Shoenfelt, E. L., Stone, N. J., & Kottke, J. L. (2018). Gaining organizational entry and developing partnerships for applied research and experience: A perspective from industrial-organizational psychology master's programs. *Journal of Industrial and Organizational*

Psychology: Perspectives on Science and Practice, 11, 606–612. https://doi.org/10.1017/iop.2018.122

Shultz, K. S., & Kottke, J. L. (1997). The master's thesis in applied psychology training. *Teaching of Psychology, 23*, 166–168. https://doi.org/10.1177/009862839602300307

Society for Industrial and Organizational Psychology, Inc. (2016). *Guidelines for education and training in industrial-organizational psychology*. Bowling Green, OH: Author.

Taylor, M. S. (1988). Effects of college internships on individual participants. *Journal of Applied Psychology, 73*(3), 393–401.

Tett, R. P., Walser, B., Brown, C., Simonet, D. V., & Tonidandel, S. (2013). The 2011 SIOP graduate program benchmarking survey Part 3: Curriculum and competencies. *The Industrial-Organizational Psychologist, 50*(4), 69–89. https://doi.org/10.1037/e559272013-007

Trahan, W. A., & McAllister, H. A. (2002). Master's level training in industrial/organizational psychology: Does it meet the SIOP guidelines? *Journal of Business and Psychology, 16*, 457–465. https://doi.org/10.1023/A:1012881209342

Troper, J., & Lopez, P. D. (2009). Empowering novice consultants: New ideas and structured approaches for consulting projects. *Consulting Psychology Journal: Practice and Research, 61*(4), 335–352. https://doi.org/10.1037/a0017843

Waldman, D. A., & Korbar, T. (2004). Student assessment center performance in the prediction of early career success. *Academy of Management Learning & Education, 3*(2), 151–167. https://doi.org/10.5465/amle.2004.13500529

Zelin, A. I., Lider, M., Doverspike, D., Oliver, J., & Trusty, M. (2014, October). Competencies and experiences critical for entry-level success for I-O psychologists. *Industrial and Organizational Psychology: Perspectives in Science and Practice, 7*(1), 65–71. https://doi.org/10.1111/iops.12108

Zhao, H., & Liden, R. C. (2011). Internship: A recruitment and selection perspective. *Journal of Applied Psychology, 96*(1), 221–229. https://doi.org/10.1037/a0021295

Zickar, M. J. &, Gibby, R. E. (2007). Four persistent themes throughout the history of I-O psychology in the United States. In L. L. Koppes (Ed.), *Historical perspectives in industrial and organizational psychology* (pp. 61–80). Mahwah, NJ: Erlbaum.

5

The Thesis Process in Industrial-Organizational Master's Programs

Kimberly T. Schneider and Morrie Mullins

The capstone requirement of many industrial-organizational (I-O) master's programs is the completion and defense of a thesis project. The thesis project is a very worthwhile undertaking; however, both faculty and graduate students sometimes struggle with issues related to student progress in completing the thesis, including supervision dynamics, Institutional Review Board (IRB) requirements, and data source options. In this chapter, we discuss the objectives that may be met and the competencies developed via an I-O thesis project, in addition to discussing potential obstacles. Based on over 35 years of combined experience in master's education, we are aware of both the benefits gained and the obstacles that graduate students encounter when pursuing a thesis; we will describe strategies that help students meet their goals and complete thesis work.

Thesis Requirements, Purposes, and Objectives in I-O Programs

Program listings on the Society for Industrial and Organizational Psychology (SIOP) website (SIOP.org) provide useful information for potential graduate students surveying programs and determining where to apply to graduate school. In late 2018 (retrieved Nov. 4, 2018), we reviewed I-O master's program data reported on that site with a focus on determining the extent to which a thesis is required, optional, or not required. After removing duplicate listings, we had data for 144 programs, including those housed in both psychology and business departments as well as online programs. We included programs from all countries of origin and programs across a variety of terminal degrees (e.g., MA, MS, MSc). There was a fairly equal split

Kimberly T. Schneider and Morrie Mullins, *The Thesis Process in Industrial-Organizational Master's Programs*
In: Mastering Industrial-Organizational Psychology. Edited by: Elizabeth L. Shoenfelt, Oxford University Press (2020).
© Society for Industrial and Organizational Psychology. DOI: 10.1093/oso/9780190071141.003.0005.

of programs that require a thesis (34.7%) and those that explicitly do not require a thesis (38.9%), with slightly fewer programs with an optional thesis (or choice between thesis or internship; 26.4%). These proportions remain relatively unchanged since Shultz and Kottke's (1996) review of I-O terminal master's programs (n = 48), although the number of programs in our review tripled in the intervening 22 years. The majority of I-O master's students are required or may opt to complete a thesis project (combined, 61.1%).

Based on the applied nature of the I-O field, some may question the relevance of a thesis requirement, particularly given that many I-O practitioners write and communicate in less formally structured ways on the job. We argue that this viewpoint focuses too narrowly on the finished thesis product and overlooks the usefulness of individual steps in thesis completion that develop critical competencies (discussed immediately below) that can be used in both academic and applied settings. Shultz and Kottke (1996) wrote that those who do not complete a thesis project have lost the opportunity to demonstrate their training and experience in designing, conducting, and communicating research. As Bray (1991) noted, the research training, methodology, and statistical skills of an I-O psychologist distinguish us from those holding master's degrees in business administration, who typically gain less substantive methodological training. In work settings, partly due to training in methodology, I-O master's graduates are more likely to fill a specialist or research role than are MBA graduates, making the thesis project closely linked to their eventual work. In fact, I-O graduate alumni from one program emphasized that the thesis developed their organizational skills, written communication, problem solving, verbal communication, and organizational "survival skills" (Shultz & Kottke, 1996).

Theses and the Demonstration of I-O Competencies

Writing a thesis is more than an academic exercise. It is also a way for students to further develop competencies that are important in their future careers. Although competencies are covered in more detail in Chapter 3 in this volume, we would be remiss not to discuss them in the context of the thesis.

A series of *The Industrial-Organizational Psychologist* articles documented the results of a competency-related survey in which respondents from consulting, industry, government, and academic backgrounds were asked to rate a large number of competencies on their importance to their respective fields. The results of the survey have since been summarized in a white paper (Zelin, Lider, & Doverspike, 2015) available on SIOP's website.

The first and most obvious thesis-related competency is writing. Zelin et al. (2015) reported that, within the consulting domain, written communication was the third-highest-rated competency for individuals in the consulting manager and expert individual contributor tracks, and the highest-rated competency for individuals simply identifying themselves as individual consultants. The *only* job category within consulting in which written communication skills did not make the top 10 competencies (out of almost 60 rated) was the consulting manager of managers. The emphasis on written communication competencies was somewhat less in industry, falling in the top 10 only for individuals classified as individual contributors or expert individual contributors, but it was a top-five competency for *all job categories* in the government sector (Zelin et al., 2015). Clearly, written communication skills matter.

The obvious counterargument is that academic writing and writing for clients and other stakeholders are very different activities and, potentially, different skillsets. We actually agree with this point. However, our students must recognize that there is no such thing as "one size fits all" when it comes to writing. A successful I-O psychologist must be able to write well for different audiences. Not all clients and stakeholders will want rigorous scientific details—but some will. Some, based on their background or prior experience with using data to support their interventions, will want documentation that provides defensible levels of scientific rigor. Students who have written a thesis will have practiced their scientific "voice" and will have the ability to shift into a more technical style of writing if the situation requires it. Thesis students will have writing-related competencies that students who have not completed a thesis simply lack.

Beyond written communication, a number of the common competencies that repeatedly appear in the SIOP white paper (Zelin et al., 2015) also are served by the thesis process. Verbal communication, for example, is important in almost every nonacademic career path I-O master's students might pursue and is developed both in meetings with the thesis advisor and in any required proposal and defense meetings. Critical thinking—the top competency overall for industry, number three overall for consulting, and number four overall for government (Zelin et al., 2015)—is relevant at every stage of the thesis process. Ethical behavior, attention to detail, accountability, and many other highly rated competencies across applied fields can all be further developed through the writing of a thesis. Although critical competencies related to ethics and accountability would presumably be part of a master's-level education in I-O psychology regardless of their links to a required thesis project, the thesis should further develop these competencies.

A final competency that is not obvious or universal, but is still important, is what can be learned from a "failed" thesis. Many students will experience false starts at various stages of the process. They might begin writing and find that the topic either no longer excites them or has been so thoroughly researched that the question they planned to study seems to be a settled issue. Perhaps more challenging is the situation in which students negotiate data collection with an organization (an ideal many students express as a goal, without understanding the logistics of such an undertaking) only to have the data collection either fail to materialize or fall apart once it is in process. And finally, students may be challenged with reconsidering or expanding a proposed framework in order to integrate conclusions from unsupported hypotheses.

Failures at or around the data collection stage provide a unique learning opportunity for students, and frequently for their mentors. As Boss and Sims (2008) reminded us, "everyone fails!" Dealing with setbacks and developing appropriate emotion regulation strategies when faced with unexpected challenges is a competency that, although not necessarily reflected in the dimensions described by Zelin et al. (2015), is vital in life.

Theses and the Development of Research-Related Knowledge, Skills, Abilities, and Other Characteristics

Although conducting formal academic research may not be part of the career trajectory of many I-O master's graduates, I-O psychologists are inherently researchers who are called upon to identify and answer applied questions with empirically defensible solutions. Nowhere is this clearer than in the 2018 update to SIOP's *Principles for the Validation and Use of Personnel Selection Procedures* (hereafter *Principles*; Sackett et al., 2018), wherein variations on the word "research" appear more than 100 times. For example, "Any claim of validity made for a selection procedure should be documented with appropriate **research evidence**" (Sackett et al., p. 4, emphasis added). Clearly, I-O psychologists do not simply provide advice; we provide data-driven solutions informed by current best practices. As such, a research background is critical.

Conducting a thesis provides a rigorous framework within which to develop skills in research design, as well as quantitative and/or qualitative analysis. These are often the skills that make master's students more competitive for PhD programs (Littlefield, Buxton, Bucher, Simon-Dack, & Yang, 2018), should they choose to apply after completing a terminal master's program. Beyond these obvious research-related skills, conducting a thesis provides students with a content area for which they have a significant depth of knowledge that exceeds what the general I-O population possesses, and that can be helpful in interviews and in their future careers. Applied jobs may require a research presentation as part of the screening process to demonstrate research-related competencies that are important on the job; students who have completed a thesis will have a nontrivial advantage in such interviews.

Perhaps most importantly, the thesis provides project management experience. In both applied and academic I-O careers, students will be called upon to manage a variety of projects. Creating a project plan, setting deadlines, following up with various constituencies, organizing materials, collecting data to provide an empirical answer to an important question, presenting information effectively and efficiently, and showing proactive leadership are all tasks that graduate students complete as part of the thesis process—and abilities they will repeatedly need to demonstrate once they begin their careers. Whether we think about it in terms of competencies or knowledge, skills, abilities, and other characteristics (KSAOs), completing an empirical thesis has a variety of beneficial outcomes for I-O master's students.

Ensuring Feasible and Appropriate Thesis Projects

Typically, when students begin a graduate program, if they are not assigned an advisor, they will speak with various faculty members to determine who might be an appropriate thesis advisor. Assuming the student has not yet identified a specific area of interest for the thesis, this is followed by choosing a topic, starting a literature review, formulating research questions, and choosing appropriate methodological and statistical strategies to examine hypotheses. Perhaps concurrently, the student and faculty advisor must consider the availability of participants or archival data, possible payment of participants, costs of obtaining materials, and, if collaborating with an organization, the potentially long process of negotiating study logistics. Once the study is planned, next steps involve choosing other thesis committee members, setting and conducting a proposal meeting, carrying out the project, and preparing to report the project results both in a written document and at an oral defense.

There are many steps, particularly in the initial stages of choosing a thesis topic, that tend to bog students down and slow their progress. Faculty have diverse approaches to supervising this process: Some faculty requiring students to develop their own research questions whereas others prefer students to work on existing projects within their program of research (Shadish, 1994). The latter approach has the advantages of enabling students to begin as early as possible, making efficient use of faculty time and resources, and potentially increasing the chance that the final product will be publishable.

Some I-O master's students develop thesis projects with organizational applications, and they may propose using organizational samples. Applied data collection could include collaborating with an external organization, working with one's own academic institution (e.g., using faculty, staff, or graduate assistants as the basis for an employee sample), using Amazon's Mechanical Turk (MTurk) or other paid data sources to obtain samples of workers, or using archival data. There are certainly benefits and drawbacks to each of these sources; we highlight a few here, with an emphasis on precautions to consider given the relatively short timeline for thesis data collection.

Collaborations with Organizations

Many I-O faculty have connections and networks within organizations, potentially making field research an enticing option for students. For students and faculty interested in developing thesis projects that are reliant on generating new data from either an external organization or their own academic institution, several common roadblocks exist. We agree with the observations of Shoenfelt, Stone, and Kottke (2018), who noted that projects involving data collection in organizations tend to be more successful if the content of the project is of top priority to the organization, prompting their motivation to see the results; the project has an internal champion at a high level; the organization already has the data readily available; or the faculty member has successfully consulted with the organization in the past.

Obstacles typically occur when there is a need to "sell" the project to the organization, the data involve sensitive content (and, relatedly, the organization's legal team must give approval of each step), data collection requires significant employee time or resources (e.g., time away from work, apps or links to collect data that may violate firewalls), or the timing of the project is unfortunate. In some cases, nonprofit organizations may be more receptive to collaborations. We have worked on such projects in the past and agree with Islam, Lahti, and Chetta (2018) that nonprofits often value research-based interventions due to their familiarity with grant-writing and their recognition of the need for I-O services but have limited funding to pay for these services.

These potential roadblocks are not always apparent at the outset of a thesis project, but one or more obstacles are likely to be encountered, requiring the faculty–student team to be flexible. Flexibility with project design and implementation has to be balanced with the rigor required of a thesis project. If changes are necessitated after the thesis proposal has been approved, many constituents (e.g., committee chair and members, organizational entities) may need to be involved to approve modifications to the project. However, we emphasize that the resultant organizational data generally are well worth the difficulties encountered because of the applied, practical implications that may follow from the results. As we noted earlier, challenging organizational projects where the student must adjust goals or parameters are an important learning experience because this type of challenge is representative of the problems encountered and the flexibility required of many I-O practitioners.

MTurk/Crowdsourcing

Recently, I-O psychologists have expanded their use of data sources such as MTurk (Cheung, Burns, Sinclair, & Sliter, 2017). Thesis students may consider such sources in an attempt to increase efficiency, access, and convenience in collecting thesis data. Although we have not yet seen empirical articles specifically focused on difficulties or advantages of reliance on MTurk data for thesis projects, there are general discussions related to data quality (cf. Harms & DeSimone, 2015; Woo, Keith, & Thornton, 2015).

MTurk can provide a diverse sample in terms of both demographics and organizational sectors (although not necessarily representative ones; Paolacci & Chandler, 2014). However, students and faculty should be aware that

MTurk data will require significant, intensive screening and data-cleaning procedures. Researchers are able to specify qualifications of participants (e.g., demographic characteristics, work status, country of origin) to target certain populations, but studies that list minimal or no restrictions for participants result in data that are often collected at suspiciously lightning-fast speed. In the case of one thesis student, over 200 working employees' attitudinal data were collected less than four hours after posting on MTurk; however, much more time subsequently was spent on data-quality checks. In another case, a thesis student quickly collected data from nearly 300 participants, but over half of the sample had to be deleted based on attention and quality checks. Significant time for data cleaning should be built into the student's timeline, including time to analyze both the closed- and open-ended attention checks that should be incorporated into all MTurk studies.

Archival Data

Archival data include data repurposed for a thesis project from sponsored research by various agencies (e.g., Pew, Gallup), government archives (e.g., Bureau of Labor Statistics), academic records, and organizational databases (Barnes, Dang, Leavitt, Guarana, & Uhlmann, 2018). Archival data can be a rich data source, including longitudinal data (e.g., General Social Survey), attitudinal and behavioral measures, as well as organizational (i.e., macro-level) outcome measures.

We recommend the toolkit developed by Barnes et al. (2018) that includes a discussion of how to best use micro-organizational (i.e., individual level) archival data. They described strategies to evaluate measurement and construct validity limitations. Regarding micro-organizational topics, there are great benefits associated with archival data that include potentially improved external validity, statistical power associated with large-scale samples, and an ability to examine context effects and engage in theory testing at higher levels of analyses.

The Institutional Review Board Process

In most universities, anyone conducting human subjects research is required to obtain approval from an IRB. The amount of time required for IRB approval and what the IRB requires will vary from institution to institution. Sometimes, these requirements can create a nontrivial barrier to finishing a thesis. Our primary piece of IRB-related guidance, based on advising many theses and the second author's 10 years as an IRB chair, is to keep both the research and the review processes easy. After describing points related to the development of the IRB protocol, we will also offer our thoughts on the potential for IRB overreach.

Keeping It Easy

A protocol submitted to an IRB can be reviewed at one of three levels—full board review, expedited review, or exempt review—with each level progressively requiring a less time-consuming examination of the research protocol. As you move down the categories—from full board review to exempt review—it becomes progressively easier to obtain IRB approval. There are ways to design a study that make the IRB review process much simpler to navigate, as we will discussed next.

Studies that require full board review will take longest to receive IRB approval because they must be reviewed in a convened meeting of the IRB. The initial review will usually occur anywhere between a week and two months (or more) after the initial submission to the IRB, depending on the IRB workload. Because most IRB submissions require some number of revisions, which must also be reviewed by the IRB, the time from submission to approval for studies requiring full board review may be anywhere from weeks to months.

Although the estimated time for an IRB review and approval may seem prolonged, the good news is that most of the studies conducted as I-O master's theses are unlikely to require full board review. Full board review is reserved for studies with vulnerable populations (e.g., children, prisoners, individuals with cognitive impairments) or studies that present more than minimal risk to participants. We see very few, if any, I-O thesis projects using minors (although studies of emerging adults, including high school student workers, are exceptions), and most I-O master's students are unlikely to conduct research on prisoners (or, frankly, will not realize a study such as evaluation of prison job training for reintegration is a thesis option). Most of the time, I-O research tends to avoid vulnerable populations.

If a study does not require full board review, the next level of review is the expedited review process. "Expedited" sounds fast and, compared to full board, it generally is. Protocols reviewed as expedited do not require the full IRB to meet to discuss the proposed study; the federal regulations require that the IRB chair, or one or more experienced reviewers designated by the chair, review the protocol. The decision to approve can be made without a board vote (though disapproving a study would have to be done by the full IRB, should that be the expedited review outcome). The efficiency of an expedited review is attractive with regard to getting started on a thesis project. There are number of categories of research projects that can be reviewed as expedited; there were nine such categories at the time this chapter was written, but these are subject to periodic updating. The easiest way to find the current list of expedited review categories is to search for the Office of Human Research Protection (OHRP)'s most recent listing using search terms such as "OHRP expedited review categories."

The fastest way to move through the IRB process, in general, is to design a study that can be reviewed as exempt. Most IRBs still require that detailed materials be submitted to their office for studies that fall into one or more exempt categories; thus, planning a study that you believe is exempt does not mean that it does not need to go to the IRB.

The vast majority of studies likely to be conducted by I-O students fall into one of the OHRP exemption categories. In early 2019, the Code of Federal Regulations (CFR) was updated, resulting in an expanded set of exemption categories such that even more of the types of studies I-O students conduct potentially qualify for exemption. Because the exemption categories are important in guiding students toward research questions and designs that will avoid IRB snags, we will describe several of these categories. The language quoted comes directly from the 2019 version of the CFR (https://www.hhs.gov/ohrp/regulations-and-policy/regulations/45-cfr-46/index.html).

The first exemption category is for pedagogical research, conducted in educational settings and involving "normal educational practices." Pedagogical research generally is not relevant for I-O theses, although some studies (e.g., on training design or delivery) may use classroom environments. The second exemption category captures many I-O theses because it encompasses research involving "educational tests . . ., survey procedures, interview procedures, or observation of public behavior" as long as participant information is recorded in a way that protects participant identity, any incidental disclosure of participant responses would not create any risk for the participants, or participant information is recorded in a way that identification is possible but the study has undergone limited review by the IRB (which may be very similar to an expedited review process). Most survey studies I-O students might conduct for their theses would likely fall in this category.

A new exemption category, as of 2019, is one that involves a "benign behavioral intervention" that coincides with data collection from an adult participant in the form of either written or verbal responses, or audiovisual recording with permission. There are some additional restrictions in this new category. However, this is an important change; prior to the 2019 revisions, any research that involved an intervention almost automatically required expedited review, potentially including manipulating survey instructions or comparing perceptions of two different scenarios (e.g., job advertisements) because the previous version of the CFR did not allow for manipulations of any kind in exempt research. To qualify as a "benign behavioral intervention," the intervention must be "brief in duration, harmless, painless, not physically invasive, not likely to have a significant adverse lasting impact on the subjects, and the investigator has no reason to think the subjects will find the interventions offensive or embarrassing."

The other exemption category that may be relevant to an I-O master's thesis is the aforementioned use of archival data, which the CFR refers to as "secondary research." Archival data that include identifiable private information may be used and qualify for exemption if (a) the information is publicly available or (b) the information is recorded by the investigator "in a manner that the identity of the human subjects cannot readily be ascertained" either directly or indirectly, and there will be no attempt to contact or re-identify the participants. There are two other circumstances that we will not cover here because they typically are not relevant to I-O student research. Each IRB should have a thorough listing of all of these exemptions as part of its application materials.

In summary, then, students who conduct the following three types of studies should qualify for exempt-status review: anonymous survey research; experimental or quasi-experimental research using a benign behavioral intervention; or archival research. Submitting such studies will often lead to a quicker and easier review of the thesis project.

IRB Oversight and IRB Overreach

Gunsalus et al. (2006, 2007) noted that IRBs have become overwhelmed by required procedures and documentation, resulting in "many protocols receiv[ing] exaggerated review" (Gunsalus et al., 2006, p. 1441). IRBs may include design-related elements in their review process that appear unrelated to the protection of human participants. As Gunsalus et al. (2006) noted, such tendencies toward "mission creep" on the part of IRBs can reduce researcher buy-in, potentially undermining the compliance system.

On the whole, concerns about research design are outside the boundaries of what must be reviewed in order to protect research participants from foreseeable harm. However, we must remember that the core guiding principles of human subjects review have to do with protecting the rights and wellbeing of all participants and making sure that all participants are treated with dignity and respect. Viewed through this lens, poorly designed research arguably is an IRB issue. Substantive design changes as a result of IRB review should be made if those changes positively impact the experience of the participants and result in increased protections for participants (potentially including increased respect). However, design decisions have generally been made based in part on prior research history. In many cases, if the researcher can present information showing that the proposed methodology has not created harm in past studies, the IRB often will allow the study to proceed as designed.

The vast majority of IRBs want to support the responsible conduct of research. Although IRBs exist to protect participants, they also protect both the university and its researchers, should an adverse event occur. These responsibilities are why some IRBs err on the side of caution, too much oversight, or even overreach (Gunsalus et al., 2006, 2007). This IRB mission creep is not because IRB members enjoy "wielding power," but because they are trying to protect multiple constituencies, with their first responsibility the protection of research participants.

On-Time Completion of Thesis Projects

One of the most challenging aspects of completing a thesis often has little to do with the content of the thesis project itself; rather, students frequently are challenged by the compressed timeline in a two-year master's program. When we consider that students are tasked with developing a research project, collecting data (or accessing archival data), analyzing and interpreting results, writing drafts, and scheduling and conducting proposal and defense meetings, all while completing their course curriculum and possibly working as a graduate assistant (or in part-time jobs) in addition to work–life balance issues, the challenge can seem daunting. In addition, master's students are asked to begin their thesis work quickly to stay on track for graduation within two years; at the same time, they are relatively unfamiliar with the I-O content area, and some may not have even completed an undergraduate I-O course. Students must be prepared to quickly get up to speed as content experts on their thesis topic.

In the initial steps of choosing a thesis topic, we recommend students have an honest discussion with their thesis advisor related to priorities and goals for the project. Students should develop a realistic timeline that reflects both ongoing academic and personal obligations. As noted earlier, faculty vary in whether they encourage students to develop their own thesis idea or to build off the faculty member's research (Lei, 2009). Our students report that thesis ideas often arise from classroom discussions in seminar courses, as well. Beyond interactions within their own master's program, students may note calls for papers in I-O journals that point toward vital areas of study; guest speakers and conference attendance likewise can spark ideas for thesis research. Students sometimes are advised to choose a topic interesting enough to hold their attention for several years; however, for some students, pragmatism rather than passion may be a priority.

We are proponents of attempting to reduce ambiguity related to the breadth and depth of a thesis project. We suggest that, early in the process, students review several recently completed theses from their program. Past theses provide concrete examples of structure and format as well as the complexity of statistical analyses. Students should also familiarize themselves with university requirements for thesis content and format, which may be provided in an online template. If departmental policy allows, there are benefits to first-year students attending I-O thesis proposal and defense meetings in preparation for their own. Volunteering to serve on any thesis-related awards committees likewise would provide access to top theses from the prior year that might serve as helpful examples.

Once thesis work has begun, students may report that advisors fail to schedule regular meetings for the purpose of checking progress. However, because the student is the "project manager" in this situation, the onus for scheduling such meetings arguably is on the student rather than the advisor. From the faculty perspective, we note the vast literature on effective feedback approaches relevant to the student–advisor dyad (cf. Lindsay, 2008). For instance, it is imperative to continued progress toward thesis completion that students leave advisor meetings with clarification on feedback, recognition of the benefits of that feedback, and a plan for acting upon the feedback (deKleijn, Mainhard, Meijer, Brekelmans, & Pilot, 2013).

In a unique quasi-experiment focused on assessing graduate student supervision during the thesis process, Dillon and Malott (1981) examined five components implemented by a faculty advisor working with 34 MA and five PhD psychology students over the course of four years: specification of research tasks, weekly meetings, deadlines, feedback, and incentives. Students earned points by attending meetings, reviewing articles, presenting data, working at least 12 hours per week to attain course credit, writing, and editing (the latter two activities were assigned greater point values). Students lost points by missing deadlines or meetings. Criteria, including committee member ratings of thesis/dissertation quality, number of articles submitted to refereed journals, percentage of students who graduated, and time to degree completion, indicated that students completed over 90% of their tasks when the point system was in effect. Interestingly, the negative point components of the system contributed nothing to thesis quality. Students rated the one-on-one weekly meeting with the thesis advisor as the most positive component of the system.

Aside from the use of regular meetings, other *structural* components can guide students to on-time thesis completion. Some programs set departmental milestones that encourage on-time completion. For instance, students may be required to develop a thesis idea by the end of their first semester, present the idea in a colloquium by a certain date, or enroll for thesis credit each semester between the proposal and defense meetings. These milestones frequently are linked to departmental policy and may be paired with punitive measures in cases where the student falls behind (e.g., a departmental assistantship may be in jeopardy if the student does not hold a proposal meeting by the start of the second year). Curriculum structure can be developed to prompt various thesis steps (e.g., literature review in a content course; research design, measure selection, or IRB proposal development in a methodology course; proposed statistical analyses with mock data in a statistics course). We have seen student success using combinations of these required milestones paired with an integration of the thesis and coursework. Faculty advisors may also use strategies that indirectly serve to increase student efficiency, such as including all advisees in a group meeting to discuss common project issues and provide social support, reducing costs for students by using common participant pools, or sharing parts of an archival dataset.

Strategies Supporting Thesis Completion

We were interested in what worked well for I-O master's graduates in completing a thesis project and included a question on the I-O master's graduate survey (Shoenfelt, 2019) that asked the following: *If you successfully completed a thesis, what were the three most helpful strategies in terms of project completion?* A total of 446 respondents provided data; we offer in Table 5.1 the number and percentage who endorsed each of the response options.

Table 5.1 Thesis Completion Strategy Ratings

Item	*n*	Percent
Having regular (e.g., weekly) meetings with my thesis chair	184	41.3
Hitting personal goals and "milestones" (e.g., completing a first draft of the literature review) in a timely manner	146	32.7
Working with my thesis chair to set goals	143	32.1
Hitting department-recommended/required formal "milestones" (e.g., forming a committee, developing a project idea) in a timely manner	133	29.8
Choosing a project that is limited in scope	131	29.4
Breaking the writing into small units, focusing on completing one section at a time	126	28.3
Focusing on relatively quick data collection or the use of archival data	125	28.0
Scheduling and blocking off specific times to write without interruptions	98	22.0
Staying on campus until completing my thesis defense	72	16.1
Writing on my thesis topic when assigned papers or projects for classes	43	9.6
Required presentation of my thesis proposal at departmental/ program colloquium	35	7.8
Keeping my committee members highly involved	32	7.2
Participating in informal student/cohort accountability support groups	12	2.7
Participating in formal thesis workshops (department or university)	10	2.2
Participating in a "thesis writing circle" or another formalized student group focused on accountability	4	0.9
Risk of losing assistantship for failure to meet proposal deadline	4	0.9

Note: Total sample size was *n* = 446

In examining the results, two themes emerged in the strategies endorsed most frequently: mentoring and goal setting. Neither of these should be surprising to anyone involved in the thesis process. The thesis is a large and, for most students, unfamiliar undertaking. Students may have written papers in the past, but few have completed something the magnitude of a thesis. As such, mentoring and proper goal setting should be key predictors of success. That 41.3% of participants indicated that weekly meetings with the thesis chair were key to thesis completion, and 32.1% reported that collaborative goal setting with their chair was key, is consistent with the published literature cited in the prior section (e.g., deKleijn et al., 2013; Dillon & Malott, 1981).

It is worth noting, however, that students indicated high levels of importance for self-set goals, with the second-highest-rated strategy (32.7% endorsed) being the attainment of personal goals and milestones. Also clear from the data is a need to recognize the thesis not as a single large document, but as a series of sections that each reflect sequential steps toward completion of the overall project. Workshops, support groups, writing circles, and more punitive strategies were least commonly selected as beneficial approaches to thesis completion by successful I-O master's students.

Concluding Thoughts

As described elsewhere in this volume and in its sister volume, *Mastering the Job Market: Career Issues for Master's-Level Industrial-Organizational Psychologists* (Shoenfelt, in press), there are many exciting career options for I-O master's graduates. We believe that the completion of a thesis serves I-O master's students well regardless of whether they intend to pursue an applied career or further their graduate training in a PhD program. Littlefield et al.'s (2018) analysis of the admissions criteria of over 220 psychology PhD programs in the United States indicated that KSAOs related to a thesis project were of either primary or secondary importance in the selection process, further emphasizing the benefits of thesis completion. Master's-degree holders who have completed a thesis can boost their credentials via highlighting details related to the thesis that are typically included in a curriculum vitae, personal statement, letters of recommendations, and interview discussions. As we have outlined, students who accept applied I-O jobs will be able to put to immediate use nearly all of the KSAOs related to the thesis.

We acknowledge that for many master's students just beginning to identify as I-O psychologists, a thesis project can be daunting. Faculty should emphasize the importance of a feasible timeline and project scope while also dissuading students from the assumption that they need to read everything about their topic before beginning to write the first thesis draft. Learning is a life-long process; we like to remind students that, like them, faculty are continually acquiring new knowledge and skills long after graduation. Reminders such as this, paired with support from faculty and their own graduate student cohort, may prompt students to begin the writing process or schedule the proposal or defense meeting, and to get on track to complete their thesis and take their next steps as I-O professionals.

References

Barnes, C. M., Dang, C. T., Leavitt, K., Guarana, C. L., & Uhlmann, E. L. (2018). Archival data in micro-organizational research: A toolkit for moving to a broader set of topics. *Journal of Management, 44*, 1453–1478. doi:10.1177/0149206315604188

Boss, A. D., & Sims, H. P. Jr. (2008). Everyone fails! Using emotion regulation and self-leadership for recovery. *Journal of Managerial Psychology, 23*, 135–150. doi:10.1108/02683940810850781

Bray, D. W. (1991). *Working with organizations and their people: A guide to human resources.* New York: Guilford Press.

Cheung, J. H., Burns, D. K., Sinclair, R. R., & Sliter, M. (2017). Amazon Mechanical Turk in organizational psychology: An evaluation and practical recommendations. *Journal of Business and Psychology, 32*, 347–361. doi:10.1007/s10869-016-9458-5

de Kleijn, R. A. M., Mainhard, M. T., Meijer, P., Brekelmans, M., & Pilot, A. (2013). Master's thesis projects: Students perceptions of supervisor feedback. *Assessment & Evaluation in Higher Education, 38*, 1012–1026. doi:10.1080/02602938.2013.777690

Dillon, M. J., & Malott, R. W. (1981). Supervising master's theses and doctoral dissertations. *Teaching of Psychology, 8*, 195–202. doi:10.1207/s15328023top0804_1

Gunsalus, C. K., Bruner, E. M., Burbules, N. C., Dash, L., Finkin, M. Goldberg, J. P., . . . Aronson, D. (2007). The Illinois White Paper—Improving the system for protecting human subjects: Counteracting IRB "mission creep." *Qualitative Inquiry, 13*, 617–649. doi:10.1177/1077800407300758

Gunsalus, C. K., Bruner, E. M., Burbules, N. C., Dash, L., Finkin, M. Goldberg, J. P., . . . Pratt, M. G. (2006). Mission creep in the IRB world. *Science, 312*(5779), 1441. doi:10.1126/Science.1121479

Harms, P. D., & DeSimone, J. A. (2015). Caution! MTurk workers ahead: Fines doubles. *Industrial and Organizational Psychology: Perspectives on Science and Practice, 8*, 183–189. doi:10.1017/iop.2015.23

Islam, S., Lahti, K., & Chetta, M H. (2018). Research partnerships between academics and consulting firms: A stakeholder analysis. *Industrial and Organizational Psychology: Perspectives on Science and Practice, 11*, 596–605. doi:10.1017/iop.2018.121

Lei, S. A. (2009). Strategies for finding and selecting an ideal thesis or dissertation topic: A review of the literature. *College Student Journal, 43*, 1324–1332.

Lindsay, S. (2008). What works for doctoral students in completing their thesis? *Teaching in Higher Education, 20*, 183–196. doi:10.1080/13562517.2014.974025

Littlefield, L. N., Buxton, K., Bucher, M. A., Simon-Dack, S. L., & Yang, K. L. (2018). Psychology doctoral program admissions: What master's and undergraduate-level students need to know. *Teaching of Psychology, 45*, 75–83. doi:10.1177/0098628317745453

Paolacci, G., & Chandler, J. (2014). Inside the Turk: Understanding Mechanical Turk as a participant pool. *Current Directions in Psychological Science, 23*, 184–188. doi:10.1177/0963721414531598

Sackett, P. R., Hough, L., Tippins, N. T., Oswald, F., Arthur Jr., W., Putka, D. J., . . . Hayes, T. L. (2018, August). *Principles for the validation and use of personnel selection procedures* (5th ed.). Bowling Green, OH: Society for Industrial and Organizational Psychology.

Shadish, W. R. (1994). APA ethics and student authorship on master's theses. *American Psychologist, 49*, 1096. doi:10.1037/0003-066X.49.12.1096

Shoenfelt, E. L. (2019). I-O master's graduate survey. Survey conducted for E. L. Shoenfelt (Ed.) (in press), *Mastering the job market: Career issues for master's-level industrial-organizational psychologist*. New York: Oxford University Press.

Shoenfelt, E. L. (Ed.) (in press). *Mastering the job market: Career issues for master's-level industrial-organizational psychologists*. New York: Oxford University Press.

Shoenfelt, E. L., Stone, N. J., & Kottke, J. L. (2018). Gaining organizational entry and developing partnerships for applied research and experience: A perspective from industrial-organizational psychology master's programs. *Industrial and Organizational Psychology: Perspectives on Research and Practice, 11*, 606–612. doi:10.1017/iop.2018.122

Shultz, K. S., & Kottke, J. L. (1996). The master's thesis in applied psychology training. *Teaching of Psychology, 23*, 166–168. doi:10.1177/009862839602300307

Woo, S. E., Keith, M., & Thornton, M. E. (2015). Amazon Mechanical Turk for industrial and organizational psychology: Advantages, challenges, and practical recommendations. *Industrial and Organizational Psychology: Perspectives on Science and Practice, 8*, 171–179. doi:10.1017/iop.2015.21

Zelin, A., Lider, M., & Doverspike, D. (2015, December). *SIOP career study executive report* [White paper]. https://www.siop.org/Portals/84/PDFs/Professionals/SIOP_Careers_Study_Executive_Report_FINAL-Revised_031116.pdf

6

Issues Faced by Faculty in an Industrial-Organizational Master's Program

Daniel A. Sachau and Barbara A. Fritzsche

In this chapter, we offer advice about the challenges faculty face as members of a terminal industrial-organizational (I-O) master's program and we discuss how faculty, particularly new/junior faculty, can deal with these issues to become productive in teaching, research, service, consulting, and shaping program culture. Think of the chapter as a collection of friendly tips for working in an I-O master's program. The tips are based on 30 years of experience directing master's programs in I-O. In addition to program administration, we have experience in university administration (as associate department chair and associate dean of graduate studies) and in directing the I-O doctoral program that is offered alongside (or in competition with, depending on your perspective) the MS program. So, we have some perspective that we can share on the view that administrators have of I-O programs. Between us, we have probably made every mistake there is to make in designing and administering a master's program and have learned a lot that we can pass on so you don't have to make the same mistakes we did!

Student Characteristics

Students in terminal I-O programs share certain characteristics that present challenges for program faculty. We will describe two general types of students that typify I-O master's students and identify challenges to faculty driven by these student characteristics. We also offer recommendations for effectively engaging both types of students. We realize that this division is an oversimplification and may be better thought of as two ends of a continuum.

Daniel A. Sachau and Barbara A. Fritzsche, *Issues Faced by Faculty in an Industrial-Organizational Master's Program*
In: Mastering Industrial-Organizational Psychology. Edited by: Elizabeth L. Shoenfelt, Oxford University Press (2020).
© Society for Industrial and Organizational Psychology. DOI: 10.1093/oso/9780190071141.003.0006.

Recent Graduates

The first category of students includes recent graduates who are looking for a program that will help them start a career. Most of these students were psychology majors. This usually means that they have a good scientific background because their undergraduate instructors emphasized research. They have often worked in labs, read journal articles, and presented at conferences, but they have limited job experience. Because they lack job experience, faculty have the challenge of helping students with job-related skills including technical writing, business dress, email etiquette, business terminology, importance of ROI, importance of social networking, résumés, LinkedIn, organizational politics, presentation skills, time management, project management, negotiation, and attention to detail.

Recent graduates understand the importance of the scientific method and know that researchers need to move slowly, be cautious, and not act until they have all the information they need. What these students do not understand is that the business world moves substantially faster than the academic world and employees need to work with a sense of urgency. Students also need to understand that business is inherently risky. Employees seldom have all the time or information they need to perfect a proposal or make a decision. In addition, the recent graduate who is admitted to a master's program was a good undergraduate student and was thus good at memorizing information, following instructions, and working within the narrow boundaries of class assignments. These students do not understand that the business world requires effectiveness in ambiguity and the ability to pivot quickly. Similarly, students from psychology programs have been taught to value science and the scientific method as the "best" way of knowing. This is, of course, a good thing, because science is what distinguishes I-O psychology practitioners from many other types of managerial consultants (Gasser, Butler, Waddilove, & Tan, 2004). However, master's students (and frankly many recent doctoral graduates) need to learn that not all managers will be convinced by a high validity coefficient or a robust meta-analytic finding. It is thus important to help students learn how to *persuade* managers using language the manager understands. Further, students need to learn that persuading managers can be difficult because many managers find intuition and experience more convincing than empirical data.

A related issue with recent graduates of psychology programs is that some of the topics we cover in master's programs may sound "fluffy" to them. Certainly, it can be difficult to quantify team building, corporate culture, or conflict resolution, but these are important issues for business leaders. Recent graduates may lack the experience that makes these topics relatable, interesting, or important. We have found that students are receptive to almost any topic if that topic is framed as a solution to a specific company's problem. This is where case studies (e.g., Harvard Business School case studies) come in handy. Faculty who do consulting can bring real-world examples to the students. If your program has an in-house consulting firm, prior projects can become good examples.

Another challenge instructors face when working with recent bachelor's graduates is these students do not yet understand the importance of playing a role on a team. Corporate projects are typically much bigger than any one person can handle alone. Freshly minted undergraduates have spent four years essentially looking out for themselves. They complete assignments by themselves and are seldom accountable to other students. It is thus important to help these students understand the importance of information sharing, collaboration, and playing a supporting role.

Here are some suggestions for serving recent graduates:

- Ask students to provide practical solutions to real-world problems as this will help them develop skills in finding theory- and research-based answers to organizational issues.
- Give students assignments where there is not one clear answer. Active learning and error-based learning develop problem-solving skills needed on the job (Bell & Kozlowski, 2010).
- Focus on developing teamwork skills (Hughes & Jones, 2011). Create assignments that are so large that no student can complete the project alone. Consider giving students grades on team, rather than individual, performance.
- Give students short deadlines for projects. This parallels real-world assignments.
- Provide students with opportunities to meet I-O professionals and encourage them to join professional organizations. Participating in local I-O, Society of Human Resource Management (SHRM), American Society of Training and Development, or Organizational Development Network chapters can enhance networking and professional skills.
- Provide students consulting experience. More on this appears later in this chapter and in Chapter 7 in this volume.

- Require an internship, as internships develop skills beyond those learned in the classroom such as professionalism, organizational savvy, and professionalism (Shoenfelt, Kottke, & Stone, 2012; Shoenfelt, Stone, & Kottke, 2013).
- Give students assignments that involve explaining science to laypeople as I-O psychologists frequently need to communicate our science to those employees in organizations who are not scientists (Thoroughgood, 2010). For example, in many classes we ask students to "explain this to me like you would to a family member."
- Require readings from trade journals and popular management books. Business leaders are much more likely have read *Good to Great* than a journal. Students should be familiar with the names of business bestsellers because their future supervisors will be talking about these books. A particularly useful exercise is to ask students to read a popular-press book on management and critique the work based on scientific theory and evidence.
- Consider creating a case competition. For example, one author's program organizes a yearly I-O Consulting Challenge. This is a three-day event where teams of students work to solve a business problem. Students from a variety of I-O master's programs are invited. Similar Consulting Challenge programs have recently been created in the Chicago and Washington, D.C. areas. Sachau and Naas (2010) provided more information about the Consulting Challenge.

Experienced Students

The second category of student who enters an I-O master's program includes experienced students who are returning to school after years away from college. These students have job experience and are pursuing a master's degree to help them change roles and/or advance in an organization. The challenge of working with experienced students is these students may have lost some of their school-related skills. It's been a while since these students have attended lectures, taken notes, read textbooks, or completed tests. Further, educational software changes quickly and they may have some catching up to do. Faculty may need to be patient with these students until they catch their stride again.

Similarly, experienced students are more likely to be "adult learners," since experience and age tend to correlate. Specifically, adult learners are generally more inclined to be driven by internal factors (e.g., how can I use this knowledge for personal change?) than external factors (e.g., what do I need to do to get a higher grade?). They tend to thrive when they can be self-directed and they learn by connecting new knowledge to their prior (and often vast) personal experiences. Thus, it is helpful to design courses and other educational experiences with this in mind (Chen, 2013).

Another challenge with students who have spent time in the corporate world is that since they graduated from college, they tend to become less concerned about science and more concerned about practice. The questions academics ask are often smaller and less practical than the questions business leaders ask (Ones, Kaiser, Chamorro-Premuzic, & Svensson, 2017). For instance, academics may ask questions simply because the process of asking and answering the questions is, well, interesting. The issue is compounded because the consequences of failing to answer a question in the academic world are less dramatic than the consequences of failing to solve a problem in the business world. This focus on practice over research becomes apparent when the more experienced students check out or push back when discussions turn theoretical, philosophical, or otherwise *academic*. It's at this point that professors need to hold their ground. Certainly we want to accommodate the experienced students, but the defining feature of I-O psychology is the reliance on *science* to solve workplace problems. Young faculty (often younger than the experienced student) may feel a bit intimidated by the senior students, but they should not let these students convince them that the scientific method, the academic journal system, and theory development should take a backseat to intuition, pop management books, and best-practice collections. To be clear, *both* the academic and practice perspectives are important.

A final challenge we have found when working with the experienced students is that although they seem to be better than the inexperienced students at managing time, they typically have less time to be involved in extracurricular activities. It may be more difficult for them to take classes during the workday. They may have home commitments that make it difficult to meet in the evenings and on weekends. They may have a harder time getting away for a three-day conference. Time constraints are particularly a problem for the senior students if they are enrolled in a program based on a cohort model.

Here are some suggestions for serving experienced students:

- Ask students to provide theoretical solutions to real-world problems. Remind students that personal experience and intuition may be the basis for many solutions in the business world, but in the world of I-O psychology—data reign.
- Ask students to include citations (in footnotes or small font) on PowerPoint presentations when they are presenting to business leaders. Students should send the message that their ideas are based on theory and research.
- Provide opportunities to meet academic professionals and join academic organizations. Students should join the Society for Industrial and Organizational Psychology (SIOP), attend the national conference, and join any local SIOP-related organizations. Students might also consider joining Division 13 of the American Psychological Association, the Society of Consulting Psychology, and/or the Academy of Management.
- Give students lab experience. We have found that once students collect and analyze data, and then start to feel competent as researchers, they become more interested in the empirical processes in I-O psychology.
- Ask senior students to teach an introductory psychology course. One of the best ways to learn a topic is to teach it. Teaching experience, like lab experience, may spark interest in an academic career.
- Ask experienced students to mentor their less experienced classmates on topics like professional dress, email etiquette, business jargon, the importance of chain of command, budgeting, profit and loss statements, time management, and so forth.
- In classes, require personal reflection and contributions from personal experience, and offer self-paced learning opportunities.
- Consider asking experienced students to teach a course or take extra courses instead of completing an internship. The internship may not be as relevant for students who already have experience in the corporate world.
- Consider moving courses to weekends or evenings. This will make it easier for working students to attend class. The downside of this is that the faculty who teach these courses may shift their workday toward evenings, and this may reduce their opportunities to interact with departmental faculty. This is particularly a challenge for young faculty who need to connect with the faculty who will vote on tenure or who have

young children or other family commitments during the weekends and evenings.

Whether your program focuses on recent graduates or experienced students, it is important to target a demographically diverse student body by admitting students from different socioeconomic status, ethnic, age, major, and gender backgrounds. For example, there's nothing like a discussion about employment discrimination and affirmative action when your students come from different protected class backgrounds! It's a wonderful learning experience for all.

Research

There are advantages and disadvantages to being a researcher in a terminal master's program. On the positive side, publication standards for master's program faculty are generally lower than for doctoral faculty. Master's faculty usually do not have to publish as many articles per year as doctoral faculty. In addition, master's faculty have a greater latitude in publication venues. For example, doctoral faculty are expected to publish in the A-level journals like *Personnel Psychology, Journal of Applied Psychology, Academy of Management Journal, Journal of Organizational Behavior,* and *Journal of Occupational and Organizational Psychology.* Master's program faculty are welcome to publish in the A-level journals but administrators will generally be happy with publications in B-level journals, specialized journals (e.g., I-O psychology applied to nursing, technology, and sports), conference proceedings, government documents, trade publications, book reviews, white papers, and magazines targeted to business leaders.

A challenge of doing research in a master's program is that teaching loads and class sizes are high relative to doctoral programs. This results in significantly less time and energy to devote to research. In addition, master's program faculty only get to work with graduate students for a few years and thus find it harder to coauthor with students than do doctoral faculty. By the time master's students develop the research skills to work more independently, they are ready to graduate. Although technical writing skills typically improve over the course of the master's program (Kottke, Shoenfelt, & Stone, 2014), students rarely write well enough to contribute as coauthors to manuscript preparation. Typically, thesis research is completed near the end of the student's time in the master's program and most master's graduates have little interest in preparing manuscripts for publication or conference presentation once they are in the workforce. Further, fewer students in a master's program get research assistantships than in doctoral programs. Thus, the financial incentive an assistantship provides for actively participating in research is less readily available for master's students.

Faculty who involve master's students in their research by providing thesis projects that are part of their research program often find this slows overall research progress. The thesis project is an excellent learning experience (see Chapter 5 in this volume; Shultz & Kottke, 1997), but it is expected that these student-led projects will have mistakes. Frequently, additional data may need to be collected or parts of the thesis study rerun before the thesis data can contribute to the faculty member's research. I-O master's faculty need to be aware of these constraints and plan research projects and completion deadlines accordingly.

Most young I-O psychology professors are graduates of doctoral programs at R1 universities (Carnegie classification: Doctoral program with high levels of research activity) and were thus socialized to value science over practice. They were encouraged to pursue jobs in doctoral institutions and to measure their success by scholarly publications, grant dollars, and editorial board memberships. When they arrive at a master's program, these young faculty have to face the reality that the teaching load, thesis assignments, committee assignments, funding priorities, consulting, and community service requirements make it difficult to maintain an A-level research program. This can be discouraging for some faculty and they start to feel like they have let down their doctoral advisors or somehow failed the scientific community. We think it is important to help young faculty see that a successful academic career in a master's program can be more broadly defined to include helping students start careers, program building, and service to government and industry through consulting.

Here are some suggestions for maintaining an active research program:

- Find collaborators both within and outside of your university. It is difficult to publish without help from others. Attend faculty networking events, receptions, and colloquia in other departments related to your research interests. Serve on relevant university committees; this will also assist in meeting your service duties and will help inform others on campus of your areas of expertise.

- Write papers based on data you have collected while working on consulting projects. Ensure you have met any university Institutional Review Board (IRB) requirements for using these data and that the data are not proprietary (i.e., you have the permission of the host organization to use their data and/or name in your paper). Some universities waive IRB requirements for data collection for consulting projects, but may require IRB approval if that collection leads to a paper submitted to a journal or conference.
- Talk to leaders in consulting firms and human resources departments. They often have large datasets and not enough time to write a paper.
- Find publication venues where you can introduce I-O psychology principles to a new audience (sports, arts, medicine, specific industries, etc.). For example, some I-O faculty have interests in sport psychology and find that the field is receptive to well-established ideas from I-O psychology. Other faculty work as consultants to, and in collaboration with, leaders in medicine. This opens the door for I-O–related publications in the medical and health care management journals.
- Choose research topics that are of interest to you. You will have to publish, but administrators will not be very concerned if the topic you study is not found in the *Journal of Applied Psychology* table of contents.
- If you are in a program with both a master's and a doctoral program in I-O, get clarity from your chair and dean about expectations for research productivity and educate them about the challenges of serving both student populations.
- Stay active in SIOP. Go to the conference. It will energize research ideas.

Consulting

Some I-O program faculty work as consultants, but there are many challenges around this practice. First, it is difficult to teach, maintain a research program, advise students, *and* build a consulting practice. Faculty should assess how much time they have available for consulting. Further, deans, chairs, and union contracts can place limits on the number of days faculty can work on consulting projects, especially if those projects take them off campus. Fortunately, administrators are more amenable to faculty consulting if graduate students are allowed to assist in the practice. We have found that master's-level students are well suited to manage employee opinion surveys and assist with market research projects, onsite training of entry-level employees, online course development, job analyses, comment coding, and literature reviews.

Using students as associate consultants is not without its complications. For example, a faculty member can work as a consultant in an official capacity as an employee of the university, or the faculty member can act as an independent consultant. If the faculty member is working for the university, then the student and faculty member are usually covered by the university's liability insurance policy. If the student is employed by a faculty member's company, the student and faculty member may need malpractice policies.

Here is a related challenge: If a student receives compensation when working as a representative of the university, compensation may limit his/her eligibility for student loans, a stipend, or an assistantship. If a student receives compensation as a subcontractor to a faculty member's private practice, the student will have a host of tax and FICA issues. As for faculty pay: If a faculty member is working as a representative of the university, there may be limits on the amount she/he can charge a client. Some schools allow faculty to charge a client a daily rate equivalent to the faculty member's daily rate on campus (total salary/contract teaching days). This rate is typically well below the going rate for independent consultants. In contrast, if a faculty member works as a representative of the university, the university will collect fees from the client and will handle all the compensation-related issues (they may keep some of the money as overhead). There is no easy answer to the question about whether it is better to consult as a representative of the university or as an independent consultant.

One of the benefits of working as a consultant is that the consultant builds strong relationships with leaders in the client organization. These relationships pave the path for student internships and employment. In addition, developing strong contacts in industry makes it easier to get access to employees for research purposes. Thus, consulting can lead to data that can be used for conference presentations, publications, and theses.

Many faculty choose an academic job over an industry/consulting job because the academic job provides greater research and teaching opportunities as well as greater control over one's time. Further, a faculty position provides a steady income so faculty can be somewhat choosier about which consulting projects they accept. Chapter 7 in this volume presents details on starting and maintaining a university-based consulting center.

Here are some strategies for managing a consulting practice:

- Check with administrators and/or the university contract to determine how many days per semester can be spent on consulting projects.
- Have all the compensation issues ironed out before you start a project. If you are working in the capacity of a university consultant, you will have to get your grants, contracts, and/or business office involved.
- Get students inside the doors of client organizations. This is an outstanding learning opportunity for students and may lead to a student internship or job. In other words, allow students to ride along for all phases of the project.
- Invite leaders from client organizations to speak on campus. This helps the students and solidifies the relationship between the client and the university.
- Ask clients if they have data on hand that might be used for research purposes. Many organizations have satisfaction/engagement survey data, 360 feedback data, and selection data but no one with free time to do an in-depth analysis.
- Bear in mind the reasons you chose academia over the corporate world. Keep the students first. Do not overload yourself with consulting work. Pick consulting projects that are interesting and energizing.

Building Program Culture and Identity

One of the joys of teaching in a master's program is the opportunity to work with students outside the classroom. We feel that faculty should encourage students to connect with their classmates and the program alumni. A student's professional network starts with classmates and people they have met during school. We also think it is important to create a strong program culture and help students identify with that culture. Here are some suggestions for building program culture and identity:

- Hold an annual offsite orientation. For instance, one of the authors take students to a resort and invites alumni to attend. The conference includes a variety of meetings (alumni talking about their careers and second-year students summarizing their internships) and fun events (boating, fishing, volleyball, etc.).

- Encourage students to travel as a group to the SIOP and Industrial Organizational/Organizational Behavior conferences. Many universities (deans and graduate college directors) have money available to support student research and conference travel, especially if the students are presenting.
- Consider a field trip to an organization that employs I-O psychology grads. For instance, one of the authors has taken students on trips to Gallup, Google, Tesla, Kohler, and SHRM headquarters. The trips help students bond and give them a common framework for discussing organizational issues.
- Develop a recurring international trip. For example, one of the authors organizes a trip every other year so that each class of students is able to participate in a trip. The trips are typically two weeks long and begin the first day of summer session. Some years, the trip is tied to the European Association of Work and Organizational Psychology conference. In other years, we find organizations to visit. Students, faculty, and the occasional alumni have traveled together to countries as varied as Ireland, Vietnam, Spain, Singapore, Germany, Ecuador, South Africa, Belize, England, and Iceland. Although these trips can be expensive, the students enjoy them and, because they are official university trips, students can apply for financial aid to pay for travel. Sachau, Brasher, and Fee (2010) provide more information about managing international trips.
- Provide office space for students. Give students keys to the space and round-the-clock access. Dedicated space provides a location for students to socialize, study, and meet for group projects. If dedicated space is unavailable, try to negotiate shared space with other programs. Some universities have dedicated space for graduate students that can be reserved. You may be able to negotiate a regular reservation for your students. If your program is fully online, use social media and university-provided learning management systems to create a web presence dedicated to accomplishing the same goals as brick-and-mortar student office space.
- Hold regular colloquia and invite speakers from across campus to present to students. This provides learning opportunities for students and builds alliances in other departments.
- Invite program alumni to judge class projects and case competitions. Many alumni enjoy coming back to campus to mentor students.
- Ask the students to organize holiday parties and cocktail hours.

- Organize a student and alumni party at the SIOP conference. Invite alumni and friends of the program to attend.
- Keep in contact with your alumni by inviting them to events. Consider developing a yearly newsletter and social media groups.
- Create an I-O psychology student organization and hold regular meetings. Have students appoint officers for the organization. Many campuses set aside money each year for official student organizations. The organization can also serve as a platform for fundraising activities supporting conference travel.
- Consider charging students an additional program fee each semester. Alternatively, some universities charge higher tuition for individual programs and the differential tuition (surplus) is used to support student programs. It is worth noting that graduates of I-O programs have starting salaries that are comparable to the graduates of MBA programs. I-O programs generally charge less than MBA programs. Students should be made aware of the value inherent in an I-O degree. This may make students more comfortable with program fees and/or somewhat higher tuition.

Managing Administrators

The first step in dealing with administrators is to increase communication with them. It is also helpful to meet with administrators to articulate your focus and gather feedback to determine how to best align program goals with university expectations. For instance, it may be worthwhile to meet with administrators to learn how your program is perceived relative to other graduate programs on campus. Keep in mind that administrators see the full range of graduate programs, from the highest-quality programs to those that are barely attracting and graduating students. You may feel that your program is of high quality, but you may be basing that judgment on different metrics than administrators focus on. And, perceptions (of both administrators and program directors) are not necessarily based on reality. When you meet with your chair, college dean, or graduate dean, pay close attention to how they describe your program. You can use that information to recalibrate their perceptions or perhaps even change your mission, depending on where the university is headed.

Some state universities are facing pressure from legislators to connect with industry and to focus on programs that lead to specific jobs. For example, in Florida, former governor Rick Scott asked all universities to make sure that 100% of students from popular majors get good jobs upon graduation in his "Ready, Set, Work" challenge (Postal, 2016). Taxpayers are somewhat less tolerant of purely academic pursuits than they once were. An I-O master's program is an ideal way for administrators to demonstrate that they are supplying the state with professionals who will fill positions in the business community. An I-O program with a consulting practice benefits the state by providing relatively low-cost services to business and government.

Program directors often face a challenge that comes in the form of pressure from university administrators who would like directors to expand their program (e.g., on-campus *and* off-campus, traditional *and* online, day *and* evening classes, 4+1 programs) and to increase enrollment (traditional *and* nontraditional students, executive *and* entry level). This pressure would be welcome if it were accompanied by greater resources, but all too often, it is not. The net effect is that faculty succumb to the pressures by increasing enrollment or expanding offerings, but the program risks losing its focus and, sometimes, its quality. To handle such pressures, it is helpful to have a clear sense of who you are as a graduate program, including your mission, target applicant, and content focus.

Here is a key issue, one that was not covered in graduate school: It is important to understand the administration's expectations for funding your program. Do you have to be profitable? Does your supervisor plan to use undergraduate tuition revenue to cover the cost of your program? Does your supervisor expect your graduate program to pay for itself? Are program faculty expected to find grant dollars? Does your supervisor expect to use the tuition from your master's program to defray the expenses of a doctoral program? It will be hard to get extra resources or keep class sizes small if your supervisor is planning to use the revenue from your program to cover the losses inherent in a PhD program.

Here are some suggestions for managing administrators:

- Think about ways that your supervisor (chair, dean, provost) can look good to her/his supervisor when your program succeeds. This might include connections to industry, student placement in prestigious organizations, consulting revenue, and drawing students from out of state.
- Do a benchmarking study to show how your master's program compares to other highly ranked competitors offering I-O master's degrees. Develop a plan for how you will compete to become a top-ranked

program and present that plan to administrators. Include in your argument how a top-ranked I-O master's program can provide much-needed services to the local business community and government organizations.

- We have found that most administrators respond well to requests for resources when the requests are supported by objective comparisons to other programs. For instance, it is easier to add a faculty member to a program when the program director can show that his/her program has fewer faculty members than most programs. Program comparisons also help when requesting changes in program credit hours, new courses, internships, internship supervision release, course loads, consulting, and assistantships.
- Administrators respond well to requests when the requests are supported by official guidelines and publications from SIOP. The SIOP (2016) *Guidelines for Education and Training in Industrial-Organizational Psychology*, the SIOP (2016) website listing of master's programs in I-O psychology, and the *SIOP Member Salary Survey* are very useful tools.
- Bring solutions to your supervisor, not just problems. It's a business cliché, but supervisors are more likely to act on your requests to solve a problem if you propose a solution at the same time you present the problem. Consider an example of needing office space: We have found that it is a good idea to scout around campus and find the space *before* you approach the dean to ask for space. That is, target unused/underused rooms on campus and then go to the dean with a specific plan for using the space. Floorplans, remodeling ideas, and space swap suggestions will help sell the idea. Think about how much easier it is for the dean to say "yes" to a complete plan than it is for her/him to create the plan. On a related note:
- Obtain dedicated space for faculty and graduate students. This will give the program an identity on campus. Administrators benefit from increasing the number of "centers" and/or programs under their direction. On a less optimistic note, an identifiable space makes a program harder to eliminate than a mere collection of faculty offices scattered across campus.
- Have a solid understanding of the mission and goals of your program. Be ready to articulate that to administrators. Focus on the positive by framing things in terms of being on target to accomplish

X, Y, and Z successes rather than focusing on asking for resources. Let administrators ask you what resources you need to meet your goals, and you will have a better chance at success if you can convince administrators that they want to be associated with your impending success than with your need to be dug out of a hole.

- Create a program advisory board and fill it with successful alumni, I-O consultants, and regional business leaders. We have found that most of the people we approach are flattered to join a board. In addition, many employees of large organizations are encouraged to make connections with academia. Hold board meetings once a year. Use that time to showcase your program's success and to ask for advice. Make certain that administrators are aware of your board and the connection with industry.

- Create a yearly newsletter highlighting your program's success. In addition to sending the letter to program alumni, mail it to senior-level campus administrators and local businesses.

- Make presentations about the success of your program to the university alumni association. If the association sees the value in your program, they will put in a good word with senior administrators. Administrators listen to the people who manage the foundation account.

- Attend college and university meetings that you are invited to, as you can learn what metrics are important and the language administrators use.

- Calculate the actual cost of running your program. Then calculate the number of class hours (tuition, number of full-time equivalency students, etc.) you need to break even. Do not convey this information to your supervisor unless you are profitable. Even if you are not breaking even, it's good to know where you stand if you ever need to justify your program at some point.

- Consider creating a radio or podcast series promoting the science of I-O psychology. The show functions as marketing for your program and helps bridge the gap between the school and the surrounding community, which are two important goals for deans. Stark, Sachau, and Albertson (2012) presented information on starting a radio show.

- There is a large disparity between the starting salaries of faculty in business schools and psychology departments. This makes it more difficult to recruit faculty to an I-O program. Program directors should point out the disparity to administrators and argue that the pay of I-O faculty should be comparable to a professor teaching management, human resource management, or industrial relations because graduates of I-O psychology programs often fill jobs in business schools.

Challenges When You Offer Both an MS and a PhD Degree

When your department offers both a terminal master's degree program and a doctoral degree program in I-O, there are certain challenges you will face in administering the master's program. The biggest challenge is in making sure that the master's students aren't viewed as "second-class citizens." This is hard to overcome. The way that one author handled it was to define our master's program as training of I-O practitioners and our PhD program as training I-O researchers. We value the scientist-practitioner model, so it seemed a good choice to direct students to our master's program if they are more interested in becoming a "consumer of research" and to our doctoral program if they are interested in becoming a "producer of research." Both are necessary, albeit different, but valued equally. We keep the curriculum separate, but we integrate students in labs, colloquia, and other extracurricular activities. Yet, we always face competition for resources (e.g., funding, space, new faculty) within the department. Fortunately, we have worked it out by having both the master's and PhD program administered by the same faculty. Even though there are different program directors with a different mission, the faculty who teach in the program are the same faculty who are invested in the success of both programs. This has turned out to be a win–win situation, for the most part. Students in the master's program feel valued. Faculty are invested. We make contributing to the undergraduate, master's, and doctoral program a requirement for achieving tenure, so even research-focused assistant professors feel a need to contribute to master's-level education. And, we present to the department as one unit, so the master's students who pay tuition and contribute to the department's student credit hours count toward the value of the I-O program to department-level metrics.

Conclusion

We feel the most important piece of advice is to know who you are, who you serve, and why you do what you do as you build your master's program in I-O.

There are many models of success. You might target I- or O-type jobs. You might build a cohort model, offer an evening program or online program, or create a 4+1 master's degree. What makes sense and what works depends on the population that you serve, your goals, your business community, and the particular culture of your university. Pay close attention to what administrators are saying, as your future may depend on their focus. Be positive in how you present your case and vision. Most importantly, avoid trying to be all things to all people, as this is a recipe for faculty burnout and program dilution.

References

Bell, B. S., & Kozlowski, S. W. J. (2010). Toward a theory of learner-centered training design: An integrated framework of active learning. In S. W. J. Kozlowski & E. Salas (Eds.), *Learning, training, and development in organizations*. New York: Routledge. https://doi.org/10.4324/9780203878385

Chen, J. C. (2013). Teaching nontraditional adult students: Adult learning theories in practice. *Teaching in Higher Education*, *19*, 406–418. https://doi.org/10.1080/13562517.2013.860101

Gasser, M., Butler, A., Waddilove, L., & Tan, R. (2004). Defining the profession of industrial-organizational psychology. *The Industrial-Organizational Psychologist*, *42*(2), 15–20. https://doi.org/10.1037/e578782011-002

Hughes, R. L., & Jones, S. K. (2011). Developing and assessing college student teamwork skills. *New Directions for Institutional Research*, *149*, 53–64. https://doi.org/10.1002/ir.380

Kottke, J. L., Shoenfelt, E. L., & Stone, N. J. (2014). Educating industrial-organizational psychologists: Lessons learned from master's programs. *Industrial and Organizational Psychology: Perspectives on Science and Practice*, *7*, 26–31. https://doi.org/10.1111/iops.12099

Ones, D. S., Kaiser, R. B., Chamorro-Premuzic, T., & Svensson, C. (2017). Has industrial-organizational psychology lost its way? *The Industrial-Organizational Psychologist*, *54*(4), 67–74. https://www.siop.org/Research-Publications/TIP/april17/lostio

Postal, L. (2016, January 18). Gov. Rick Scott challenges Florida universities to help graduates get jobs. *Orlando Sentinel*. https://www.orlandosentinel.com/news/education/os-rick-scott-universities-popular-majors-jobs-20160118-story.html

Sachau, D., Brasher, N., & Fee, S. (2010). Three models for short-term study abroad. *Journal of Management Education*, *34*(5), 645–670. https://doi.org/10.1177/1052562909340880

Sachau, D., & Naas, P. (2010). The Consulting Challenge: A case competition. *Journal of Management Education*, *34*(4), 605–631. https://doi.org/10.1177/1052562909358556

Shoenfelt, E. L., Kottke, J. L., & Stone, N. J. (2012). Master's and undergraduate industrial/organizational internships: Data-based recommendations for successful experiences. *Teaching of Psychology*, *39*(2), 100–106. https://doi.org/10.1177/0098628312437724

Shoenfelt, E. L., Stone, N. J., & Kottke, J. L. (2013). Internships: An established mechanism for increasing employability. *Industrial and Organizational Psychology*, *6*(1), 24–27. https://doi.org/10.1111/iops.12004

Shultz, K. S., & Kottke, J. L. (1997). The master's thesis in applied psychology training. *Teaching of Psychology, 23,* 166–168. https://doi.org/10.1177/009862839602300307

Society for Industrial and Organizational Psychology, Inc. (2016). *Guidelines for education and training in industrial-organizational psychology.* Bowling Green, OH: Author.

Stark, E., Sachau, D., & Albertson, D. (2012). Producing a radio show about psychological science: The story of psychological frontiers. *Teaching of Psychology, 39*(1), 42–44. https://doi.org/10.1177/0098628311430311.

Thoroughgood, C. (2010). The two-minute elevator speech: Communicating value and expertise as I-O psychologists to everyone else. *The Industrial-Organizational Psychologist, 48,* 121–125. https://doi.org/10.1037/e579012011-017

7

University-Based Consulting Centers as Part of an Industrial-Organizational Master's Program

Michael Hein, Richard G. Moffett III, and Yoshie Nakai

Students and faculty in industrial-organizational (I-O) psychology master's programs may work with business clients through a university-based consulting center (Kraiger & Simpson, 2008). A university-based consulting center is an entity housed on campus that provides internal and external consulting services. Typically, a consulting center is self-supported, and many return funds/proceeds to the university. The center is run by I-O faculty and graduate students, who are the service providers to organizational clients. Although faculty and students may provide administrative support, a consulting center might have a staff person to maintain the office and provide administrative services. The university human resources department, outreach, or grants and contracts office may perform payroll, hiring, contracting services, and/or other services. Consulting centers may be housed in an individual program or department or operated at the university level. The centers typically work with clients on various personnel and organizational development issues. Involvement in consulting center activities provides additional training for students in the affiliated I-O master's program. University-based consulting centers can provide significant returns in terms of graduate student experience, community outreach, and profitability; however, there are important considerations before an I-O program undertakes such an endeavor. A consulting center may not be feasible for many I-O programs. In this chapter, we discuss the key considerations for establishing and maintaining an I-O consulting center and implications for student development. We address issues at three levels: faculty/program, department, and university, each with different considerations for the success

Michael Hein, Richard G. Moffett III, and Yoshie Nakai, *University-Based Consulting Centers as Part of an Industrial-Organizational Master's Program* In: *Mastering Industrial-Organizational Psychology*. Edited by: Elizabeth L. Shoenfelt, Oxford University Press (2020). © Society for Industrial and Organizational Psychology.
DOI: 10.1093/oso/9780190071141.003.0007.

of a university-based consulting center. We end the chapter with practical considerations for running a consulting center.

"To Be or Not to Be" (*Hamlet*)—Is a Consulting Center a Good Fit for Your Program and Program Faculty?

The Society for Industrial-Organizational Psychology (SIOP) provides this definition of I-O psychology: "Industrial-organizational psychology is the scientific study of working and the application of that science to workplace issues facing individuals, teams, and organizations" (SIOP, 2019). This broad definition of I-O psychology provides for a variety of I-O graduate program emphases, ranging from a research orientation to an applied orientation. A consulting center is a better fit for graduate programs in which applied work is an integral part of the education and training of the students. In applied programs, consulting is more likely to be viewed as a legitimate part of a faculty's duties by the faculty members, their I-O program colleagues, the department chair, non-I-O psychology faculty, the dean, and the university leadership.

Contributions to Meeting SIOP Education and Training Guidelines

The General Knowledge and Skills area in the SIOP *Guidelines for Education and Training in Industrial-Organizational Psychology* (SIOP, 2016) indicate Professional Skills as a competency to be developed by I-O graduate students. Professional skills includes skills in communication, business/research proposal development, consulting, and project management. A consulting center can provide graduate students with opportunities to develop these important skills and can play an important role in student education and training for master's-level I-O practitioners.

In addition to the content areas and competencies to be mastered by I-O graduate students, the *Guidelines* (SIOP, 2016) identify strategies educational programs may use to develop each area of competence. In addition to traditional coursework and research activities incorporated in the core graduate curriculum, consulting entities provide opportunities for I-O graduate students to develop additional competencies such as professional skills through participation in supervised experience and on-the-job training in client projects supervised by I-O program faculty members. A potentially unique way consulting entities support the guidelines is through opportunities for modeling and observation. Models may be I-O program faculty leading projects or upper-level graduate student peers working on the same projects. Students have opportunities to observe the models, practice their skills, and subsequently pass on skills to other I-O students. For example, students who have never participated in a project contracting process may attend client meetings with the I-O faculty member. Graduate students may observe the basic process and critical behaviors that take place during the process. In a later project, the students can lead a contracting meeting with the supervision of faculty or experienced graduate students. As the students build competence, they can assist other students in developing skills.

In consulting center projects, students typically collaborate with I-O graduate student peers regardless of cohort and research group membership. This collaborative feature of a center helps students further develop their professional network within the program. A consulting entity affiliated with an I-O master's program encourages students to manage multiple roles. I-O graduate students are treated as consultants. Both faculty members and students must recognize each other as performing out of their regular role. For example, the faculty members may switch from "instructor" to a "supervisor/colleague" role; graduate student peers move from "classmates" to "colleagues."

Synergies with Internships

In an applied master's program, I-O graduate students likely want to and may be required to have an internship. Some students may be able to do their internship with a consulting center, but others likely will complete internships with local companies. The presence of a consulting center may lead to future opportunities for internships as companies learn about I-O graduate student capabilities. Likewise, internships may lead to consulting projects as companies become aware of the center's capabilities. The center leadership may lay out internship and consulting options for their clients and let the organization decide which best meets their need. With a consulting project, the client typically gets more direct faculty involvement and supervision of the project than with an internship, but this comes at a higher cost to the organization.

Is the Center Designed and Viewed as an Integral Part of the Education of Students in the Program?

Ensuring that a consulting center is designed and viewed as an integral part of the education and training of graduate students in the I-O psychology master's program provides a number of benefits. Framing a center as an important component of the I-O master's program can increase support for the center from various stakeholders. Administrators at all levels and faculty from the department and program are more likely to view faculty consulting projects in a positive light if they are pursued to help educate and train students. In one case, many of the I-O faculty were involved in consulting projects before a center was established, most of which involved graduate students, and funds were brought through the university. This history of student involvement helped the program formally establish the center as a means of educating and training students.

When a center is seen as important for educating I-O master's students, program faculty likely will be supportive of the center's efforts. This support can come in multiple forms. Faculty may lend their expertise and provide supervision of students on projects, which require significant expenditure of time and effort. Faculty members who do not directly provide support as a consultant can provide support in others ways (e.g., carrying a heavier load for thesis supervision, teaching additional courses), as they see the work of the center benefiting the education and training of the students.

Departmental support may be gained by demonstrating to the department chair and faculty members that faculty involved in the center are "team players." For example, the center can assist the department through pro bono projects such as facilitating departmental strategic planning or conducting a needs analysis for one of the department's programs. Another welcomed way a center can assist the department is through financial support, especially if consulting center project proceeds are not already formally shared with the department. In one example, a center covers half the cost of the department's copier costs beyond the cost of the center's use of the printer. Another center provides financial support for undergraduate psychology majors to attend meetings of their regional psychological association and for the department's psychology club.

It is important to determine the reporting structure for a center and to have the support of the academic entity in which the center is located. In one instance, a senior leader of the university advised the center leadership to avoid intradepartmental politics by reporting to the college dean rather than within the department. This reporting structure avoided conflict within the department and assisted in gaining the support of the department chair and colleagues, which was important for the success of a center. The center leadership may consider how the center contributes to the department and communicate the non-negotiable factors. That is, it is important that support for the consulting center does not come at the expense of the department, other graduate programs, or the undergraduate programs. This may include not cannibalizing faculty lines, graduate assistantships, or other types of support. Again, it is important to emphasize how the center promotes the academic standards of the department and the I-O master's program. Taken together, these recommendations should help reduce departmental resistance to the idea of a consulting center.

Finally, if administrators see the center as a key component of the education of students, they may be more likely to support the center. Administrators may be tempted to view the consulting center as a profit center for the university or as an income generator for faculty. However, center leadership should help administrators recognize that the center is aligned with the academic mission of the university.

Do the Mission, Vision, and Values of Your Center Align with Your University, College, Department, and Graduate Program?

Having the right mission, vision, and values is critical to the success of any organization, including a university-based consulting center (Grant, 2016). It is important that the mission, vision, and values of the center align with and further the mission, vision, and values of the I-O psychology graduate program. In one instance, an I-O graduate program vision was to be one of the top applied master's I-O psychology programs in the United States. Involving students in applied projects (e.g., class projects, consulting projects) was a key education and training component of this program vision. The idea for a center evolved out of this program vision as it was seen as a means to help take the program to the next level, a top applied I-O psychology master's program. In addition, the center leaders ensured that the work of the center was aligned with the strategic goals of the university to enhance academic achievement, nurture a student-centered learning environment, and establish partnerships with external organizations. In this case, aligning with the strategic goals of the university was instrumental in securing approval and start-up funding for the center from the university administration.

An alternative approach to mission, vision, and values may be less formal and more evolutionary. For example, another I-O psychology master's program idea for a center evolved out a consulting project by an I-O faculty member and I-O graduate students. To accommodate such projects, the university worked with the faculty member to develop a consulting entity to handle the contracting and funds generated by such consulting projects. Thus, the center developed from this administrative need. No formal process was used to establish the mission, vision, and values for the center; they evolved organically and informally.

Program Changes

Program-level changes may pose challenges to continuing a consulting center. For example, a master's program may transition from a brick-to-mortar to a fully online format. Such a program-level shift leads to changes in student needs and program resources devoted to a consulting center. In a fully online program, many students have a full-time job and may not be consistently available to work on a consulting project. Students likely are geographically dispersed and may not be available to meet with local clients. The scope of the center must be realigned with the master's program, department, college, and university. Center stakeholders may use the center's mission and vision as a guide to develop new strategies in a realignment process. For example, the center may collaborate with the department to actively recruit upper-level undergraduate students who can participate in the center's activities through cooperative education or practicum. Modifications such as this could enhance the educational value of a consulting center beyond the I-O master's program.

Faculty Expertise, Skill Development, and Readiness

Operating a consulting center as part of an I-O master's program has clear and direct positive effects on student learning; however, there are indirect effects on faculty, as well. The rationale for a faculty member engaging in applied work can involve a number of professorial duties. Active consulting faculty are connected to the applied practice of I-O psychology. Faculty experiential learning can be returned to the classroom as conducting applied projects informs classroom teaching, especially when teaching I-O psy-chology topics. Applied experiences can bring to life the material in a text-book and increase faculty members' credibility in the eyes of the students. For example, faculty can draw upon their experience in conducting job analyses to teach the challenges of applying this technique in organizations. Courses can be continually updated to reflect current practice and lessons learned in the field. For example, several years ago, one of the authors re-ceived a call from an existing client asking if we could develop an onboarding process for the organization. After assuring the client that we could, the fac-ulty consultant and a project associate (I-O graduate student) researched best practices in onboarding. Onboarding as a topic was subsequently integrated into the graduate training and development course. Applied experience can help sharpen faculty consulting skills and can help them become better role models/supervisors for students engaged in class projects where applied experiences are integrated into classroom learning (O'Neill & Jelley, 2014).

Applied work may lead to applied research questions and opportunities to conduct research in organizations for faculty or for graduate student theses. Although consulting may lead to situations where a faculty member can collect field data that could be used for research purposes, generally faculty complete fewer research projects when they are actively consulting. When deciding whether or not to start a center, research expectations at your uni-versity should be considered. Starting a center with primarily untenured faculty could be a very risky venture. We recommend waiting until there is a core group of tenured I-O faculty before attempting to start a consulting center. Substantial administrative work is required to start a center, such as establishing contracting processes, managing budget accounts, getting students hired, determining how to compensate faculty, obtaining space and equipment, developing a website, establishing the organizational structure, and marketing services. Much of this work would not count toward tenure and promotion decisions at most institutions.

"To Thine Own Self Be True" (*Hamlet*)— Setting Your Center up for Success

Do You Have Support from University Stakeholders?

It is critical to the success of the consulting center to have the support of university leadership—the president, the provost, and other university executives such as a vice president for outreach and/or a vice president for business. Each of these stakeholders controls resources (e.g., space, funding for start-up or continuing financial support, approval of contracts) that are vital to the work of a center. To gain administrator support, I-O faculty must demonstrate the value of the center. In our experience, it is useful to indicate how the center can be an important component of the education and training of I-O master's students. For example, share information from SIOP that supports the applied nature of the field and how supervised field experiences are important to educating I-O psychology graduate students (i.e., *Guidelines for Education and Training in Industrial-Organizational Psychology*; SIOP, 2016). Aligning the mission of the center with the strategic goals of the university should resonate with top university leaders who are sensitive to these goals. Administrators may view promoting university outreach as a center responsibility. For example, projects that help local and state businesses and organizations can be highlighted to external university stakeholders as examples of how the university contributes to their community. Centers can conduct projects for their respective university governing boards, such as systemwide surveys, organizational analysis, leadership development, and scorecard development. These are high-profile projects that the university leadership can promote as a valuable service to the members of the governing board.

Does the University Have the Infrastructure to Support a Center?

The university must have the infrastructure to support the work of a consulting center for the center to be successful. A critical factor is start-up funding because it likely will take some time to complete enough consulting work to provide funding for things such as a faculty line or funding adjunct positions to cover release time for center leadership, assistantships for graduate students, and overhead for items needed to run a center (e.g., computers, printers, supplies, phones). In one example, a center received start-up funding from the university president for the first five years on a phase-out where less support was provided every year with the expectation that the center would be self-supporting after five years. Other centers have used different strategies. One center used the funds from an initial consulting project as start-up funds. Initial overhead costs were kept to a minimum as they continued to build their start-up funds with each new project until sufficient funds were developed to invest in expanding their infrastructure (e.g., space, renovations, equipment).

Other infrastructure support likely will be required from university departments such as a contracts office, accounting services office, and human resources department. Each of these departments plays a critical role in helping a center function. The success of consulting centers depends heavily on the support of these university offices and, if they are resistant, fail to see the value of a consulting center, or have slow and burdensome processes, a consulting center will not flourish and may not survive.

Depending on university policy, faculty consulting may not necessarily have to come through the university. Many I-O faculty consult without bringing the work through an on-campus consulting center. An advantage of being on campus is that you have the assistance of the university bureaucracy in conducting some of the administrative work involved in a center. Hiring center staff, payroll, liability insurance, and contracting with organizations are among the major activities that can be made easier by being internal to the university. There are perceptual advantages both on and off campus for consultants being affiliated with a campus-based consulting center rather than a faculty member's "side hustle," such as name recognition, prestige, and credibility. A potential disadvantage of being on campus is that you are required to work through university bureaucracy to get things done, and universities are not always designed for speed and efficiency. In addition, some universities charge non-negotiable indirect costs or a "service fee" of up to 30% of income, which may result in a higher price for the organization for consulting activities.

"We Must Take the Current When It Serves, Or Lose Our Ventures" (*Julius Caesar*)—Practical Considerations for University-Based Consulting Centers

Are There Enough Potential Clients in Your Area to Sustain a Center and Can You Market Your Services to Them?

An important consideration is the geographical location of the university and the number of businesses and industries (i.e., potential clients) located in the area. Although it is possible to consult virtually, most consulting contacts are developed through relationships, which are easier to develop and maintain in person. Virtual consulting projects may be limited in the type and scope of work. Virtual projects may limit the educational experience for students, especially regarding developing client management skills. Many consulting projects require significant face-to-face time with clients. If a consulting team has to travel a significant distance to meet with clients and conduct the project, expenses may become prohibitive and the project may not be feasible with the academic obligations of students and faculty.

The location and number of potential clients also affect the marketing of the center's services. We found marketing center services is best accomplished through in-person networking that can be accomplished in a number of ways. First, referrals by university leaders to other campus entities can be an effective way to create initial clients. One center secured projects for the university president's office such as strategic planning for the president's cabinet and leadership development for faculty. This initial work led to other campus entities and university system members learning about the center, expanding the potential client base and resulting in more projects. Second, local I-O psychology-related professional organizations (e.g., local I-O psychology groups, Society for Human Resource Management, Association for Talent Development) could be a rich source of referrals. Making presentations to these organizations, serving on their committees, and serving on their board of directors can provide networking opportunities. Third, you may consider leveraging the I-O program's existing business relationships. Past internship sites can be a source of networking for clients. Center faculty may want to partner with the program internship director to market for internships, consulting projects, and applied class projects to various organizations. Finally, program alumni can be a rich source for referrals, both to colleagues in their own organization and to members of others in their professional network. Program alumni know the capability of the program and consulting center and can serve as effective and credible advocates for the center's expertise. In general, we have found that consulting services are most successfully marketed by relationships and reputation. Some clients find the center because you are affiliated with the university or are referred by program alumni. However, one of our center's best sources for marketing is repeat business from satisfied clients.

"Brevity Is the Soul of Wit" (*Hamlet*)—Proposal and Contracting Process

Consulting centers typically use a written proposal and a formal contract when providing services to organizations. The process usually starts with an initial client meeting where we, as consultants, listen to the clients to try and understand their need. If we feel the identified project is a fit for the center, we draft a proposal to outline the services we could provide and a cost estimate for the services that we then send to the prospective client as a draft. We make it clear that the proposal is a working document and is our best attempt to communicate what we heard from them and how we think we can address their need.

The contracting process can make or break a consulting center. There are universities and clients who seemingly cannot process a contract in less than six months. This timeframe can be a great detriment to the consulting process because clients generally come to you when they realize they have a need for help and are not willing to wait six months to get started. To streamline the contracting process, the center leadership must maintain a good working relationship with the business and finance entities at the university such as the vice president of business and finance, the university legal counsel, and the purchasing office. In one instance, a center developed a boilerplate contract form that could be used for most consulting situations and that ensured the university would be in compliance with relevant laws. The center worked with the university purchasing office to put the contract form online for submission and approval. This process resulted in center contracts without substantive changes to the boilerplate generally gaining approval within days; contracts with changes requiring review by the contracts office or legal counsel were generally processed within weeks rather than months. This streamlined process helped to ensure contracts were not lost because of bureaucratic delays on campus.

The Nuts and Bolts of Dollars and Sense

The center fee structure is an important consideration. We recommend modeling the center's service fee structure similar to many I-O consulting firms. For example, one center charges an hourly rate for the work of faculty and pays the faculty member at half of the rate. This differential is the primary source of overhead funds to pay for the costs of the center. The center charges an hourly rate for students with a smaller surcharge for overhead. The student pay rate is competitive with the best-paying local internship opportunities.

An absolute financial requirement for an on-campus center is that the center be allowed to carry over funds from one fiscal year to the next. Many departments on academic campuses have been the victim of "use it or lose it" administrative policies regarding funding. The center is likely to have contracts that span the fiscal year deadline; money from those contracts must be available to pay faculty and graduate students to complete the work that has been contracted.

Generally, there tends to be an ebb and flow to consulting work that is difficult to predict. This inconsistent income stream can be a significant stressor, especially if the center has committed to funding graduate students. In some ways, an on-campus center is uniquely suited to this situation. Center base operating costs are low, and there is a flexible group of students available to be hired onto projects as work becomes available. Ideally, a center would be allowed to build up a reserve fund to cover down times. For instance, one center maintains one year of operating expenses in reserve to weather a downturn in consulting contracts. This center survived the 2007–2008 recession by using its reserves to make payroll. One author, through consultations with several university-based consulting centers, identified as a major stressor pressure from university administration to pay typical indirect costs at federal government grants rates. In our experience, it is not possible to pay center consulting staff at a competitive rate and bid projects at a competitive rate if the center is required to incorporate these high levels of overhead. A self-funded consulting center essentially is a small business, which must run as lean as possible to stay in business. We strongly believe students should be paid for their work, especially when faculty are being paid. When organizations request consulting projects that offer high potential student learning experiences but do not have money available to pay, we refer these requests to applied class projects where the graduate students are working for academic credit (Hein & Moffett, 2019). Nonprofits and small companies often fit into this category.

People Make the Place

For virtually any consulting entity to be successful, it is necessary to have a core group of people to carry out the day-to-day business operations, despite the noted ebb and flow of consulting projects. In one instance, a center started with five years of funding for two I-O graduate assistant positions and was expected to fund students on their own after that. This center hired two students from each graduate student cohort as 10-hour twelve-month project associate graduate assistants. The graduate assistants had the option of working additional hours at the hourly rate if consulting work was available and their course load allowed for it. Additionally, this center hired other I-O graduate students to work on projects on an hourly basis. The criteria for selecting graduate assistants to be center project associates are different from the criteria for selecting graduate assistants for the department. Academic success indicators (e.g., grade-point average, Graduate Record Examination scores) are still important as the students need to be successful as graduate students first and foremost. However, job and internship experience, especially dealing with internal or external clients, can be extremely valuable for graduate student project assistants.

For a center to be successful, I-O faculty must want to do consulting to provide experiential learning opportunities for their graduate students. If the motivation for doing consulting is educational, you avoid some pitfalls such as accepting an inappropriate project because the money is enticing or failing to meet client needs because the faculty member is trying to incorporate his/her research into the consulting project.

"Things Won Are Done; Joy's Soul Lies in the Doing" (*Troilus and Cressida*)—Logistics of Running a Center

Coordination of projects and personnel is an important task for the center leadership. Based on the mission of the center, the leadership may prioritize projects that allow for student involvement. Projects range from a half-day workshop to multiyear contracts. Projects may include job analysis, job redesign, recruiting, selection, training and development, performance management, organizational surveys, organization change and development, or leadership development. At times, multiple teams of I-O faculty and graduate students may be working on multiple projects simultaneously. The center leadership should maintain a project client list that includes current projects, potential projects, and completed projects that are still awaiting payment. We recommend a weekly meeting in which the project leads provide updates on the status of each project and generate a to-do list with tasks assigned to individuals.

Because of the constant built-in turnover that results from staffing the center with I-O master's students, we recommend a center rely heavily on job aids. Job aids should be created for all administrative tasks and recurring consulting work (e.g., leadership development workshops). I-O graduate students who are working with the center should train new graduate students on all the job aids used in the center. New students may learn further about the job aids by updating them as policies and procedures change.

We have a few final considerations for maintaining the professional atmosphere of a center. Appropriate job titles for students communicate a professional relationship to the clients and encourage students to have a clear sense of their role at the center. In one of the centers, all I-O graduate students are referred as project associates or senior project associates. At another center, students work as assistant or associate consultants. Development of a center logo could supplement the marketing effort. For example, the center may purchase each of the graduate students logo clothing items (e.g., shirt, blouse, or sweater) to wear to client meetings.

Conclusion

A consulting center can be a great addition to I-O master's programs. However, there are several requirements for establishing and maintaining a successful center. First, the fit between the I-O master's program and a consulting center should be carefully considered. The center leaders must evaluate their environment in terms of university support and potential clients. The center must gain the support of the administration and secure dedicated faculty who value an experiential learning model and actively engage in consulting. The center leadership should be prepared to meet its financial and business operations obligations. Finally, a center creates additional responsibilities and developmental opportunities for students and faculty. Each of the costs and benefits of a university-based consulting center must be evaluated regularly to maintain a healthy consulting entity as a part of an I-O master's program.

References

Grant, R. M. (2016). *Contemporary strategy analysis: Text and cases* (9th ed.). West Sussex, UK: John Wiley & Sons.

Hein, M., & Moffett, R. (2019). Specific outreach: Graduate classes and university consulting centers. In J. Allen & R. Reiter-Palmon (Eds.), *The Cambridge handbook of organizational community engagement and outreach* (pp. 153–164). New York: Cambridge University Press.

Kraiger, K., & Simpson, R. (2008). Establishing a university-based consulting practice. In J. W. Hedge & W. C. Borman (Eds.), *The I/O consultant: Advice and insights for building a successful career* (pp. 327–333). Washington, D.C.: American Psychological Association. https://doi.org/10.1037/11755-038

O'Neill, T. A., & Jelley, R. B. (2014). Integrating practical experience in I-O courses. *The Industrial-Organizational Psychologist, 52*(1), 142–153.

Society for Industrial and Organizational Psychology. (2016). *Guidelines for education and training in industrial-organizational psychology.* Bowling Green, OH: Author.

Society for Industrial and Organizational Psychology. (2019). *Industrial and organizational psychology: Science for a smarter workplace.* https://www.siop.org/Portals/84/SIOPgeneralbrochure.pdf?ver=2019-05-14-141936-670

Index

Tables are indicated by *t* following the page number.

For the benefit of digital users, indexed terms that span two pages (e.g., 52–53) may, on occasion, appear on only one of those pages.